T0343919

EDITORIAL

Law and the new world order

Index editor **Rachael Jolley** argues that it is vital to defend the distance between a nation's leaders and its judges and lawyers, but this gap is being narrowed around the world

48(02): 01/03 I DOI: 10.1177/0306422019858845

IT ALL STARTED with a conversation I had with a couple of journalists working in tough countries. We were talking about what kind of protection they still had, despite laws that could be used to crack down on their kind of journalism – journalism that is critical of governments.

They said: "When the independence of the justice system is gone then that is it. It's all over."

And they felt that while there were still lawyers prepared to stand with them to defend cases, and judges who were not in the pay of – or bowed by – government pressure, there was still hope. Belief in the rule of law, and its wire-like strength, really mattered.

These are people who keep on writing tough stories that could get them in trouble with the people in power when all around them are telling them it might be safer if they were to shut up.

This sliver of optimism means a great deal to journalists, activists, opposition politicians and artists who work in countries where the climate is very strongly in favour of silence. It means they feel like someone else is still there for them.

I started talking to journalists, writers and activists in other places around the world, and I realised that although many of them hadn't articulated this thought, when I mentioned it they said: "Yes, yes, that's right. That makes a real difference to us."

So why – and how – do we defend the system of legal independence and make more people aware of its value? It's not something you hear being discussed in the local bar or café, after all.

Right now, we need to make a wider public argument about why we all need to stand up for the right to an independent justice system.

We need to do it because it is at the heart of any free country, protecting our freedom to speak, think, debate, paint, draw and put on plays that produce unexpected and challenging thoughts. The wider public is not thinking "hey, yes, I worry that the courts are run down, and that criminal lawyers are in short supply", or "if I took a case to trial and won my case I can no longer claim my lawyer's fees back from the court". On an ordinary day, most of us are not in court or fighting a legal action, so it is only when we are, or when we know someone who is, that we might →

EDITOR
Rachael Jolley
DEPUTY EDITOR
Sally Gimson
SUB EDITORS
Tracey Bagshaw,
Adam Aiken

CONTRIBUTING EDITORS
Irene Caselli, Jan Fox
(USA),
Kaya Genç (Turkey),
Laura Silvia Battaglia
(Yemen and Iraq),
Stephen Woodman
(Mexico)

EDITORIAL ASSISTANT
Lewis Jennings
ART DIRECTOR
Matthew Hasteley
COVER
Ben Jennings

THANKS TO
Sean Gallagher,
Ryan McChrystal

MAGAZINE PRINTED BY
Page Bros.,
Norwich UK

INDEX ON CENSORSHIP
indexoncensorship.org | +44 (0) 20 3848 9820 | 1 Rivington Place, London EC2A 3BA, United Kingdom

ABOVE: Lawyer Sir Sydney Kentridge, who represented Nelson Mandela, fights for Saan newspaper group in court against press restrictions

→ realise that something important has been eroded.

Our rights are slowly, piece by piece, being undermined when our ability to access courts is severely limited, when judges feel too close to presidents or prime ministers, and when lawyers get locked up for taking a case that a national government would rather was not heard.

All those things are happening in parts of the world right now.

In China, hundreds of lawyers are in prison; in England and Wales since 2014 it has become more risky financially for most ordinary people to take a case to court as those who win a case no longer have their court fees paid automatically; and in Brazil the new president, Jair Bolsonaro, has just appointed a judge who was very much part of his election campaign to a newly invented super-ministerial role.

Helpfully, there are some factors that are deeply embedded in many countries' legal histories and cultures that make it more difficult for authoritarian leaders to close the necessary space between the government and the justice system.

Many people who go into law, particularly human-rights law, do so with a vision of helping those who are fighting the system and have few powerful friends. Others hate being pressurised. And in many countries there are elements of the legal system that give sustenance to those who defend the independence of the judiciary as a vital principle.

Nelson Mandela's lawyer, Sir Sydney Kentridge QC, has made the point that judges recruited from an independent bar would never entirely lose their independence, even when the system pressurised them to do so.

He pointed out that South African lawyers who had defended black men accused of murder in front of all-white juries during the apartheid period were not easily going to lose their commitment to stand up against the powerful.

Sir Sydney did, however, also argue that "in the absence of an entrenched bill of rights, the judiciary is a poor bulwark against a determined and immoderate government" in a lecture printed in Free Country, a book of his speeches.

So it turned out that this was the right time to think about a special report on this theme of the value of independent justice, because in lots of countries this independence is under bombardment.

It's not that judges and lawyers haven't always come under pressure. In his book The Rule of Law, Lord Bingham, a former lord chief justice of England and Wales, mentions a relevant historical example. When Earl Warren, the US chief justice, was sitting on the now famous Brown v Board of Education case in 1954, he was invited to dinner with President Dwight Eisenhower. Eisenhower sat next to him at dinner and the lawyer for the segregationists sat on his other side. According to Warren, the president went to great lengths to promote the case for the segregationists, and to say what a great man their lawyer was. Despite this, Warren went on to give the important judgement in favour of Brown that meant that racial segregation in public schools became illegal.

Those in power have always tried to influence judges to lean the way they would prefer, but they should not have weapons to punish those who don't do so.

In China, hundreds of lawyers who stood up to defend human-rights cases have been charged with the crime of "subverting state power" and imprisoned. When the wife of one of the lawyers calls on others to support her husband, her cries go largely unheard because people are worried about the consequences.

This, as Karoline Kan writes on p23, is a country where the Chinese Communist Party has control of the executive, judicial and legislative branches of government, and where calls for political reform, or separation of powers, can be seen as threats to stability.

As we go to press we are close to the 30th anniversary of the Tiananmen Square killings, when thousands of protesters all over China, from all kinds of backgrounds, had felt passionately that their country was ready for change – for democracy, transparency and separation of powers.

On an ordinary day, most of us are not in court or fighting a legal action, so it is only when we do, or we know someone who is, that we might realise that something important has been eroded

Unfortunately, that tide was turned back by China's government in 1989, and today we are, once more, seeing China's government tightening restrictions even further against those who dare to criticise them.

Last year, the Hungarian parliament passed a law allowing the creation of administrative courts to take cases involving taxation and election out of the main legal system (see p34). Critics saw this as eroding the gap between the executive and the justice system. But then, at the end of May 2019, there was a U-turn, and it was announced that the courts were no longer going ahead. It is believed that Fidesz, the governing party in Hungary, was under pressure from its grouping in the European Parliament, the European People's Party.

If it were kicked out of the EPP, Hungary would have in all likelihood lost significant funding, and it is believed there was also pressure from the European Parliament to protect the rule of law in its member states.

But while this was seen as a victory by some, others warned things could always reverse quickly.

Overall the world is fortunate to have many lawyers who feel strongly about freedom of expression, and the independence of any justice system.

Barrister Jonathan Price, of Doughty Street Chambers, in London, is part of the team advising the family of murdered journalist Daphne Caruana Galizia in relation to the Maltese government's failure to hold an independent inquiry into her death.

He explained why the work of his colleagues was particularly important, saying: "The law can be complex and expensive, and unfortunately the laws of defamation, privacy and data protection have become so complex that they are more or less inoperable in the hands of the untrained."

Specialist lawyers who were willing to take on cases had become a necessary part of the rule of law, he said – a view shared by human-rights barrister David Mitchell, of Ely Place Chambers, in London.

"The rule of law levels the playing field between the powerful and [the] powerless," he said. "It's important that lawyers work to preserve this level."

Finally, another thought from Sir Sydney that is pertinent to how the journalists I mentioned at the beginning of this article keep going against the odds: "It is not necessary to hope in order to work, and it is not necessary to succeed in order to hope in order to work, and it is not necessary to succeed in order to persevere."

But, of course, it helps if you can do all three. ⊗

Rachael Jolley is editor of Index on Censorship

BELOW: Australian journalist Peter Greste and his Al-Jazeera colleagues, Egyptian-Canadian Mohamed Fadel Fahmy and Egyptian Baher Mohamed, wait to hear the verdict of their trial for allegedly supporting the Muslim Brotherhood on 23 June 2015

CONTENTS

VOLUME 48 NUMBER 02 – SUMMER 2019

CREDIT: Ben Jennings

PICTURED: A woman painted with the colours of the Venezuelan flag listens to National Assembly president Juan Guaidó, in Caracas, Venezuela, on 1 May 2019, a day after members of the opposition clashed with government forces

CREDIT: Miguel Gutierrez/EPA-EFE

SPECIAL REPORT

≡ JUDGED: How governments use power to undermine justice and freedom

Turkey's rule of one

This year's mayoral elections in Turkey have been testing the country's checks and balances. **Kaya Genç** looks at the growing anxiety about the lack of separation of powers

48(02): 08/10 | DOI: 10.1177/0306422019858476

MINUTES BEFORE TURKS broke their fast on the first day of the Muslim holy month of Ramadan, Turkey's supreme electoral council ordered a re-run of the 2019 mayoral elections in Istanbul.

Five weeks before, the Istanbul election was won narrowly by an opposition candidate, and observers had hoped that President Recep Tayyip Erdogan's ability to cope with an opposition in Istanbul was a good sign for the future of the country. The council was ruling on an appeal by Erdogan's Justice and Development Party (AKP). For those who wondered whether the country retained separation of powers a year after implementing a new presidential system, the Turkish judiciary's apparent subservience to the government now provided a clear answer. It did not.

Next year, Turks will celebrate 100 years since Turkey's parliament opened its doors for the first time but, as that historic day approaches, the country retains little separation of its powers.

If judges and prosecutors only follow the constitution, which says the judiciary must be independent and impartial, we will be able to breathe a sigh of relief

As executive president, Erdogan heads Turkey's largest political party, handles foreign policy and enjoys the support of three-quarters of the Turkish media, which is run by loyalist tycoons.

Employees of the national news agency Anadolu and the public broadcaster TRT receive their paycheques from his office, and all key appointments in the judiciary are made from the presidential palace. Lawmakers complain that the parliament has become a ghost building and lost its significance. But although the president appears to have parliament, the media and the courts under his thumb, 2019 has emerged as the year that his one-man rule started to be challenged.

The real challenge emerged during the mayoral elections. Erdogan held 102 rallies over 50 days during that campaign, but his party lacks any other charismatic politicians, and victories were won by opposition parties in Turkey's most prosperous and largest three cities.

But in the aftermath of the elections, problems caused by the concentration of power in the presidential palace came to the fore.

First, Anadolu, which broadcast results on election night, faced a conundrum. The difference between mayoral candidates in Istanbul was smaller than three-tenths of one percentage point, and the opposition candidate was winning. In order not to upset the government, Anadolu's director, a former adviser to Erdogan, stopped updating the results. By noon the next day, Anadolu still refused to publish the outcome, but that position soon became untenable.

A week later, Turkey's governing party applied to the high election board for a re-run of local elections. An even bigger dilemma emerged as the AKP proposed a live-streamed recount of ballots in front of the TRT cameras.

As they waited for the board's decision, many Turks were left in the dark about the political machinations. Would state institutions function without prejudice? Did the judiciary actually have independence?

There were some indications of change. In April 2019, shortly after the mayoral elections, a pro-government columnist proposed that mayors should be appointed without elections, because they slowed down Turkey's progress. The Ottoman Sultan Abdul Hamid II, who closed the fledgling parliament and took over control in 1878, is being celebrated as an ideal statesman by some.

On 25 April, cartoonist Musa Kart and half a dozen other journalists from Cumhuriyet, Turkey's oldest newspaper, were imprisoned, handing themselves into authorities, after appeals against their convictions for terrorism-related charges failed. Then on 2 May, the Turkish constitutional court found that arrest and detention of Cumhuriyet journalists Akın Atalay, Murat Sabuncu, Ahmet Şık (now an MP) and Bülent Utku did not violate their rights to freedom of expression and liberty. Turkish prosecutors accused the journalists of aiding both the Gülen religious movement,

which the government blames for the 2016 coup attempt, and the Kurdistan Workers' Party (PKK). Şık previously published a book criticising the Gülenist movement.

Alican Uludağ, a star legal reporter on the newspaper, also fell victim to this crumbling of powers. In 2017, his reporting about a prosecutor resulted in a 10-month prison sentence; last year, during the trial of an American pastor imprisoned in Turkey, Uludağ's reporting on political interference in the court case again got him into trouble. A police investigation charged him with "denigrating the Turkish state".

Uludağ finds the disintegration of Turkey's separation of powers alarming. "There is no judicial independence or impartiality in Turkey," he told Index. "Instead, the government controls courts which silence journalists who scrutinise power. Judges and prosecutors act like members of the ruling party."

He points to how synchronised the executive and the judiciary have become. "Members →

ABOVE: Supporters of Istanbul Mayor Ekrem Imamoglu clash with police during a protest in May 2019. The mayor from a Turkish opposition party narrowly won the election and now the supreme electoral council has ordered it be run again

When the judiciary can't protect itself, it can't protect journalists, either

→   of the judiciary talk admiringly about this synchronisation," he said.

This is not unprecedented. Multi-party politics began in 1950 after six centuries of sultanates, with intermittent attempts at representative democracy. The Ottoman Parliament opened for the first time in 1877 and was shut down a year later. It reopened in 1908, and was shut down again in 1920.

Although Turkey's current parliament opened in 1920, it took three decades to implement a multi-party system with free elections. The current opposition party, the CHP, held power for the republic's first 30 years.

When the AKP rose to power, in 2002, its leaders advocated to transform Turkish politics along European lines, and pledged to build a system of checks and balances. Sixteen years later, there is little trace of these promises.

In Uludağ's view, the erosion of the separation of powers strips legal protections from Turkish journalists and he says a "climate of fear" hangs over the judiciary.

"Judges and prosecutors fear expulsion or exile," he said. "When the judiciary can't protect itself, it can't protect journalists, either."

Uludağ believes the judiciary faces a choice: "They can act as defenders of the government, which took a hit during the elections, or they can clear this climate of fear by protecting freedoms."

Turkey's problems with its separation of powers have been long in the making. In 2016, the EU's Turkey rapporteur, Kati Piri, proclaimed: "There is no separation of powers between the government and the president", adding: "A system without any checks and balances at a moment when we see those political developments and at the same time that the rule of law is deteriorating in the country is certainly not bringing Turkey closer to Europe."

Since 2006, an independent German foundation, Bertelsmann Stiftung, has been analysing the health of democracies worldwide. Its 2018 report found that the country where separation of powers was the most worrying was Turkey.

In 2019, it ranked 109th in a list of 113 countries in the World Justice Project's Rule of Law Index.

Ironically, the AKP was founded in 2001 on a critique of Turkey's democratic deficit and its lack of separation of powers. The leaders of the AKP called themselves conservative democrats, pledging to fight Turkey's anti-democratic foundations.

But a decade ago the party's tone began to shift.

"Since Erdogan's clash with Shimon Peres in 2009's World Economic Forum over Israel's offensive against Gaza, we clearly saw the emergence of a new AKP," Taner Doğan, a member of the Chatham House think-tank and an assistant professor from Ibn Haldun University, told Index.

As part of his doctoral studies at City University, London, Doğan examined shifts in the AKP's political communication strategies between 2002 and 2017, through interviews with party officials, think-tanks and academics close to the government.

In Doğan's view, Mohamed Morsi's ousting in Egypt, the Gezi Park protests in Turkey in 2013, and a failed coup attempt against Erdogan in 2016 altered the party's language.

"The lukewarm support of Western countries during the coup became serious ammunition the government used in election campaigns. Nowadays, belief in democracy in Turkey is waning fast, and Erdogan's symbolic ascension to leadership of the Muslim world is built on a political narrative countering Israel, Western democracies and the international media."

But Uludağ remains hopeful and says separation of powers is "as vital as bread and water". In his view, the way out of the current crisis is simple: "If judges and prosecutors only follow the constitution, which says the judiciary must be independent and impartial, we will be able to breathe a sigh of relief." ⊗

Kaya Genç is a contributing editor for Index on Censorship, based in Turkey

England, my England (and the Romans)

Author **Robert Harris** draws on history to discuss power and how democracy must prevail with **Sally Gimson**

48(02): 11/14 | DOI: 10.1177/0306422019858477

"**A**LMOST ALL MY** books are about the power of information and the struggle to control information," said Robert Harris, one of Britain's best-selling authors.

We are discussing his novels, the problems for democracy and free speech around the world.

"It seems to me," he told Index, "that democracy is a form of channelling of power – almost like a system of dykes and sluices, you know, so that it doesn't flood: it's controlled. At the moment you move to something like referendums, or you allow unbridled use of technology, all those old methods of control have gone."

Harris is a political author, which is rare in Britain today. His novels are often based in other centuries, but the problems of power are similar. He started writing about Nazi Germany, but his Cicero Trilogy – Imperium, Lustrum and Dictator – concentrates on ancient Rome and his most recent novel, Conclave, centres on the election of a new pope.

He sees similarities between what was happening in Rome during the time of Cicero and the rise of strongman leaders today. "The thing that destroyed the Roman republic was the oligarchs whipping up the masses against an elite who had previously sat in control. You may say that's a good thing, but the lesson from the Roman republic is [that] you can destroy democracy and then it vanishes from the earth for 1000 years or so," he said.

"If we go back to the Romans, my image of power is something like plutonium, something radioactive, you know. It's a great dynamic force, but if you touch it for too long, or hold it [for] too long, it will destroy you."

He believes power needs to be broken up, so that it is not abused. "It has to be diffused through a judiciary, it has to be diffused through a free press, it has to be diffused through elected institutions," he said. "There are lots of things which are all very slow and often can become corrupt, with all sorts of problems to them, but in the end they provide safeguards so that no one has the power of the dictator to say that we will do this."

We are eating fish and chips in a pub near his home in Berkshire. This is rural England, as the English like to imagine it – green rolling fields, warm beer and ancient Anglican churches, where change seems to happen slowly, if at all. Harris lives in the old rectory nearby. It could be a million miles away from London, but this area is part →

Power is something like plutonium, something radioactive ... if you touch it for too long, or hold it [for] too long, it will destroy you

RIGHT:
Author Robert Harris

→ of what is called the "home counties", and the capital is only an hour away by train. It is a perfect place for a writer, particularly one who is interested in the intricacies of power. It is near enough the centre to entertain people from the heart of government – he mentions a recent conversation with a cabinet minister – but just far enough away to be able to write undisturbed.

Recent history is also on his mind. "There was a complete high-water mark after the Berlin wall came down," said Harris. "There was this belief that democracy could simply be transplanted from the West all over the world – the whole of eastern Europe, Russia, the Middle East, Africa – and all the fruits would flow and everyone would be like us: freedom of speech, property rights and so on. But, of course, one realises that it is immensely more complicated than that and, actually, 'one person, one vote' is potentially an instrument of tyranny."

As he explains, the power of the simple majority is a terrifying thing for the minority on the other end of it.

"And what we have got, or were supposed to have, is a system that protected minorities, so unless there was a great consensus for some change voted on in elections along with a range of other concerns, you couldn't make a sweeping change. Things moved slowly. It was a kind of Burkean view."

CREDIT: Dan Kitwood/Getty

For someone who has thought of himself as a "man of the left", this is rather extraordinary and Harris goes on to talk about Edmund Burke, a Whig politician of the late 18th century whose thinking was shaped by his revulsion at the chaos caused by the French Revolution, and whose ideas are at the core of traditionalist Conservatism today.

Harris says he now believes, as did Burke, that there is a wisdom and collective strength in institutions that predate us, and will last after we have gone.

"I believe in liberal institutions, I suppose. I see them as a guarantee of our freedom. Wherever you do away with those institutions, or challenge them, [loss of] freedom of expression quickly follows."

He is convinced, he says, from writing his book Conclave, that the Catholic church's slow and exhaustive way of choosing the next pope is why that institution has survived so long.

"To my surprise, having long been what I would have thought radical in my views, I have now come to entertain serious doubts about this, because you could have a plebiscite which says: 'We want political control of the judiciary. Why shouldn't the judges, a classic elite, out of touch, be elected? They should come under political control. It's an outrage.' And then off we go with the usual things about immigration, or deporting Islamic militants or anything." And, he says, we change our minds, when people who we like are deported, and it is too late.

He says that democracy should be slow and deliberative, and that democracy and freedom look like people "arguing endlessly in a way a lot of people find frustrating" while dictatorship is often hailed as being dynamic. Therein, he believes, lies the danger.

"One of the most useful books I have ever bought was a 1936 Baedeker guide to Germany produced for the Olympic Games. It has a section on modern history at the beginning describing the Third Reich in neutral terms and one of the things it says is that: 'National Socialism came to power to put an end to fruitless parliamentarianism' like it's a good thing." he said.

An acute observer of politics, Harris has often been bruised by it. His admiration for British Prime Minister Tony Blair was shattered by the way Blair behaved over the Iraq war. Now he is witnessing Britain divided by a referendum. He says that the debate on Europe is fundamentally about what Britain is: "Not just about whether we are Europeans, but what sort of democracy we live in."

He says that debate is being shut down and people are becoming intolerant of any other point of view. "The thing is, today, you have to be careful what you say," he said, adding that when he was growing up, such caveats did not apply.

"In many ways it is good you have to be careful what you say. The vast change in my lifetime towards sexual minorities and ethnic minorities, is wholly good, but few things in the world are ever entirely good.

"So, if you were to say anything in defence of [US President Donald] Trump or Brexit in certain circles you would have to be careful →

OPPOSITE:
English circuit court judges gather at Westminster Abbey in London in October 2018 ahead of the annual church service to mark the start of the legal year. The service dates back to the Middle Ages and is attended by more than 700 judges and senior judicial figures

Harris says he now believes, as did Burke, that there is a wisdom and collective strength in institutions that predate us, and will last after we have gone

13

Promis'd Horrors of the French INVASION, —or — Forcible Reasons for negociating a Regicide PEACE. Vide. The Authority of Edmund Burke.

It is immensely more complicated than that and, actually, 'one person, one vote' is potentially an instrument of tyranny

→ in a way that I don't think you would have had to have been 20 years ago – and equally on the other side. I know one of the things that has powered Trump, and has powered Brexit and the right, is the idea people can't tell the truth and [say that] 'This area has totally changed'. That this is *verboten* by the authorities . That's badthink. That's a thought crime."

He is frightened, too, that in some universities people can no longer say things for fear of offence. "The totalitarian thing of saying: 'tear down this statue, it offends me'," he said. "The world then becomes, as in the Orwellian nightmare, just the present and whatever the dictates of the present are – the past is removed.

"So, I'm no lover of Cecil Rhodes, but it seems crazy that you should pull his statue down, or take down the statue of Nelson or any other commander, that you have a kind of 'year zero' approach to culture and history."

He continued: "I think that freedom and challenging institutions is a *sine qua non* of democracy, but when you say that to even hold such thoughts on either side is forbidden then we are in dangerous waters. So, each

side has to recognise the validity of the other's arguments."

Harris's latest novel, The Second Sleep, due out in September 2019, is, in part, about words being forbidden. He has been correcting proofs the day we meet. The dystopian novel, he says, looks at what happens when a society such as ours, reliant totally on technology, collapses and people have nothing to fall back on. They repudiate technology and head to the church, which becomes a focus of life.

"In my dystopia, the church exercises control through the 12,000 words of the Bible and that is the language. And although a few other words can be used, by and large the science is gone and the world is controlled through language."

But, says Harris, he feels that he is lucky. He will not be locked up for what he writes.

"When I wrote my novel about the election of the Pope, which I really enjoyed doing, there was a moment when I sat here in the comfort of west Berkshire and thought: 'Here I am, I am writing the most subversive novel imaginable about a religion with more than a billion followers around the world. I'm going into its most sacred ritual and I am writing about it and no one is going to criticise me.

"'There won't be any denunciations in The Guardian, there certainly won't be any physical threats.' I thought if I did this about another world religion first of all my publisher might turn it down, secondly I would be denounced, and thirdly I might well require a policeman on the gate. It brought home to me that even just what I do, as a novelist of entertainment, there are forces out there … and when it comes to physical violence against you, or against your family, then everything looks very different.

"That's where we have been fantastically fortunate here. All my life, and I'm 62, I've been able to say whatever I like." ⊗

Sally Gimson *is deputy editor of Index on Censorship*

ABOVE: Promis'd Horrors of the French Invasion by the English artist James Gillray. This cartoon from 1796 shows the bloody consequences invoked by politician and philosopher Edmund Burke if the French revolution was played out on the streets of London. Magna Carta is being burnt and acts of parliament have been designated "waste paper"

"It's not me, it's the people"

Mexico's new government promised it would start rebuilding the nation's pillars of democracy but, says **Stephen Woodman**, old habits die hard

48(02): 15/18 I DOI: 10.1177/0306422019858479

IN HIS ELECTION campaign, Mexico's new president, Andrés Manuel López Obrador, promised to tackle the country's freedom of expression crisis, address the erosion of government transparency and bring major change to a country mired in corruption.

His landslide victory in July 2018 humiliated the Institutional Revolutionary Party (PRI), which ruled for 77 of the past 90 years. But has anything changed, or has López Obrador forgotten his early promises to start rebuilding Mexico's democracy?

The hopes of many activists and media workers were raised when the veteran leftist politician won the election. Strengthening the role of the media would be in line with a pledge to improve Mexico's democratic values and would be seen as a signal of the new president's commitment.

Nearly a year later, details are still emerging about the manipulative strategies the former government used to cling to power for so long. Although the PRI paid lip-service to press independence, its officials routinely resorted to bribery and intrusive surveillance measures to keep potential opponents in check. The question is: is López Obrador going to make the significant changes that are necessary to address this and other democratic practices?

While the new president has promised to halve official advertising spending during his six-year term – a move the global freedom of expression organisation Article 19 hailed as positive – he is beginning to show signs of having little time for the media's role as a watchdog.

López Obrador often uses his daily media briefings to criticise the "*fifí*", or snobby press –particularly the national outlet Reforma. In April, he demanded the newspaper reveal the source of a leaked government letter, arguing that transparency was not "just an obligation for the government but for everyone". After an outcry, the president stopped applying pressure.

But the following week, he issued an apparent threat to the press. "If you cross the line, well, you know what happens, right?" he said. "But it's not me. It's the people."

The president said his comments had been misunderstood and he was not intending to create fear of reprisals. However, he stopped short of an apology.

"It is very concerning that the maximum authority in the country is undermining journalists," said Gabriela Rasgado, a reporter from the eastern state of Veracruz. "He calls us everything except objective."

Mexico is the deadliest country in the Western hemisphere for journalists. So far, López Obrador has offered little in terms of concrete measures designed to protect media workers.

In fact, Rasgado believes the president is fanning the flames of this crisis. She recently discovered that a state government press officer was calling her radio station and asking about her work. Shortly after, the station stopped publishing her reports relating to state politics. Rasgado filed a police complaint and told the president about the harassment after one of his daily briefings. "That doesn't happen anymore," was his reply. After publishing →

Details are still emerging about the manipulative strategies the former government used to cling to power for so long

→ a video of the testy encounter on Twitter, Rasgado was subjected to an online smear campaign. Supporters of the president said she had taken bribes from the previous government and was angry that they had stopped – an unproven claim she categorically denies.

Many other journalists have been subjected to similar attacks since López Obrador's inauguration. In February, Guadalajara's ITESO university published a report showing a network of Twitter users and bots were taking aim at journalists for perceived slights on the president. The study showed national reporters who covered the morning conferences were most likely to be targeted.

But Rasgado said that local reporters, rather than political correspondents, would ultimately bear the brunt of this intolerance. According to the Committee to Protect Journalists, 95% of those killed for their work in Mexico between 1992 and 2017 reported for local outlets. As a journalist working in Veracruz, Rasgado covered the 2010-16 term of governor Javier Duarte. During that period, 17 reporters were killed in the state. Now she worries that López Obrador's behaviour could inspire copycat aggression.

"This [hostility] sets an example that is replicated by state governors and wider society," Rasgado told Index. "If we are going to face six years of this, I don't want to know what will happen."

When López Obrador took office in December, media outlets mostly welcomed the change in leadership style. While the previous president, Enrique Peña Nieto, rarely spoke off-script, the new president invited questions from journalists at daily morning conferences.

However, Genaro Lozano, a Reforma columnist, told Index the move highlighted López Obrador's desire to dominate the media narrative.

"It's all about him," Lozano said. "You turn on the news and they're talking about what the president said. Media

workers and activists struggle to generate interest in other issues. It's hard to compete with such a popular and spotlight-loving president."

"Millions have put their trust in the new government," said Griselda Triana, the widow of Javier Valdez, a journalist who was murdered in the coastal state of Sinaloa. "We cannot let [the president] take a step backwards."

RIGHT: A victory rally for President Andrés Manuel López Obrador in Mexico City on 1 July 2018. The 64-year-old is the 58th president of Mexico

Triana has first-hand experience of illegal state manoeuvres. Ten days after suspected cartel gunmen killed her husband in May 2017, she began receiving suspicious text messages purporting to be from national media outlets.

The first message, claiming to be from the magazine Proceso, referenced her husband: "Prosecutors announce carjacking was the motive for Valdez murder." The next day, she received a more cryptic message, reportedly from the website Animal Politico: "What do you think about this story? When they run out of words, they resort to attacks."

In March 2019, the digital watchdog Citizen Lab revealed the messages contained Pegasus spyware created by the NSO Group, an →

ABOVE: A protester takes to the streets in downtown Mexico City in a bid to bring attention to the case of murdered journalist Javier Valdez in 2017

→ Israeli cyber security firm. If Triana had opened either link she would have unknowingly installed malware on her mobile phone. The program provides access to most of a hacked phone's functions, including the camera and the microphone.

Peña Nieto denied his government was behind the hacking attempt but admitted buying the spyware. However, the NSO Group said it sold the tool only to governments. The company stressed that Pegasus could not be transferred between devices or used by anyone except the purchaser.

Triana recalls avoiding the links and she later reported the incident to the police. She is waiting for the investigation to conclude, hoping the current administration uncovers the abuses of the past. "What is needed is political will," Triana told Index. "I am interested in the truth ... Where is this infrastructure? It was used by the Mexican government – it can't have disappeared from one day to the next."

Citizen Lab has documented 25 cases of activists, lawyers and journalists receiving Pegasus-infected messages in Mexico. The most

famous target was the broadcaster Carmen Aristegui. In November 2014, Aristegui exposed corruption at the heart of government when she revealed that Angélica Rivera, the first lady, had received a mansion from a government contractor.

Aristegui received a slew of infected messages in the months following the report. She and her investigative team were also fired from MVS Radio. The national station claimed the dismissals stemmed from a separate dispute in which the company accused two of Aristegui's colleagues, Irving Huerta and Daniel Lizárraga, of improperly associating the brand with a side project. A Mexican court later ruled the action illegal.

The scandal suggested the PRI leadership had not abandoned its old authoritarian habits. The party held power from 1929 until 2000 and silenced the press with a mixture of pressure and bribery.

"The PRI only tolerated press freedom in so much as it gave the impression that it was governing democratically," Huerta told Index.

Eighteen months after MVS Radio fired him and his colleagues, Huerta left to study for a doctorate in London. He is unsure whether he will return to work in Mexico. In fact, Huerta says his decision largely rests on whether the new administration can tackle the state interventions and violence that strangle investigative journalism in the country.

"López Obrador represents two things to me," he said. "The promise that the country can change and the fear that it doesn't." ⊗

Millions have put their trust in the new government ... We cannot let [the president] take a step backwards

Stephen Woodman *is contributing editor, Mexico, for Index on Censorship. He is based in Guadalajara, Mexico*

When political debate becomes nasty, brutish and short

The USA has long prided itself on its democracy. **Jan Fox** looks at how the constitution and the separation of powers is standing up against the onslaught from a populist president

48(02): 19/22 | DOI: 10.1177/0306422019858480

WHETHER IT'S THE US Attorney General refusing to appear at a Congressional committee or someone calling out a political rival as treasonous, the political conversation in the USA is becoming nasty, brutish and short.

Many worry that the country of some 329 million people, which has prided itself on modelling the greatest democracy in the world, is not immune to unpicking some of its checks and balances – and that this could also have profound symbolic effects around the world.

Academics are debating whether US democracy is robust enough to withstand a populist such as Trump, who likes to ride roughshod over agreed democratic norms.

A recent example was an unprecedented move in May when Trump revoked the White House press passes of a substantial number of journalists, including most of the Washington Post's reporters, claiming they had not met new standards. Journalists were told they had to seek new passes which give them less access.

Reporters from CNN, The New York Times, Buzzfeed and other media outlets were excluded from a press briefing in 2017 – a trend seen by many as a bid by the president to control the free press.

As Steve Levitsky, co-author with Daniel Ziblatt of the book How Democracies Die told Index: "The checks and balances in our government are mostly being eroded by the breaking down of 'informal norms' – the basic norms that underlie any constitutional democracy such as mutual toleration and forbearance or self-restraint in the exercise of your power."

The USA prides itself on its constitution and its system of separation of powers. The founding fathers set up a robust three branch system of the legislative (Congress), the judicial (the courts) and the executive (the president). All the branches checked each other's power to make sure no one branch dominated the other. The press is often seen as a fourth check on that balance of power.

"A constitutional democracy absolutely requires restraint of the legal powers available to Congress, the executive and the courts, which are immense in theory," said Levitsky. "The president has the power to pardon pretty much whoever he wants [and] Congress can →

ABOVE: US Capitol police stand guard behind a barricade in Washington DC

→ remove the president." He argues that this fine balance has been in the process of breaking down for decades and Trump is only the most extreme example, with "the two main parties seeing each other as enemies rather than rivals".

But it is the polarisation of politics rather than the breakdown of these systems that is dangerous, he adds. He says it started in the era of President Bill Clinton and continued with accusations against President Barack Obama.

"Trump is a symptom of polarisation not a cause. This constitutional hard-balling goes back to the 1990s and Clinton's impeachment, which had no bi-partisan consensus and violated the spirit of the law," he said. "Then there was a major increase in partisan influence with the rise of Obama, fuelled by the likes of Sarah Palin and Mike Huckabee, calling him anti-American or even [saying] that he wasn't American at all. When you describe a president as anti-American, you're saying he is potentially treasonous. And there have been many obstructive tactics employed, too – the most egregious of which was the refusal to allow Obama to fill the Supreme

The political conversation in the USA is becoming brutal and polarised

great credit, he didn't do that. Were we to have a similar attack on the US today, Trump would never show the same restraint."

The US government announcement of 17 charges under the Espionage Act, introduced during World War I, against Wikileaks founder Julian Assange, set off more alarm bells. First Amendment lawyer Floyd Abrams said: "His indictment under the US Espionage Act threatens every journalist who writes about intelligence, national security and the like and who is dependent upon confidential sources in doing so." While UCLA journalism professor Jim Newton worried about the implication for First Amendment rights.

Levitsky argues that the courts and judges show plenty of signs of independence. "The judiciary is working better than the other branches of government, adhering more to the norms of professionals and is a pretty effective check," he said. "However, the politicisation of the judiciary under Trump may mean that fewer people will trust the courts."

David Snyder, executive director of the First Amendment Coalition, agrees. "One area where we've seen the guardrails hold is the courts' check on executive power," he told Index. "Federal courts put the brakes on efforts by the president that were unconstitutional and the Trump administration complied and adjusted the Muslim travel ban.

"The path it took to the Supreme Court was what the founders of our country envisioned. Maybe we'll see a similar showdown with all the subpoenas that various House committees are issuing now. We'll see what happens if the president ignores a court order."

Snyder worries about what is happening outside Washington where this polarisation is having a tangible effect, such as in the way individual states dealt with environmental protests over →

Court vacancy left by the death of Justice [Antonin] Scalia in 2016."

He added that equating an opponent with anti-patriotism or treason was an easy tool to use. "This has been done before – back in the 1790s, during the Civil War and in the McCarthyism period – but for the most part it wasn't a problem in mainstream politics in most of the last century and politicians have not gone there," he said. "For example, after 9/11 [President] George W Bush had the opportunity to use patriotism against Democrats but, to his

There is a worrying trend from both left and right to silence and punish political views you don't agree with

→ the Dakota pipeline construction.

"After the Dakota pipeline protest there was a raft of bills in various state legislatures that we should allow criminal punishment for protest such as blocking traffic as part of a protest. The sentiment that underlies these efforts is very strong. When we lose the ability to listen to other communities it's dangerous."

Snyder also sees checks and balances threatened at a local level, where there are problems with issues such as public access to records.

"The press, especially the national press, has done terrific work in exposing what's going on at federal level, but at local level there are fewer reporters doing fewer stories and asking for information from public records. The problem that happens when those requests decline is that these federal agencies start to get into the mindset of thinking the records are theirs and not the public's."

Snyder also says polarisation is affecting debate, saying people are willing to talk only to people they agree with, which shuts down debate and can skew issues.

"No one would deny that we have to look at some of the issues we have around immigration, but it has devolved into a cartoon argument about a wall. National debate on the subject has been hijacked," he said.

Lack of open debate is affecting academic freedom, says Henry Reichman, chair of the American Association of University Professors committee on academic freedom and tenure and author of the new book The Future of Academic Freedom.

"The biggest threat to academic freedom is the narrowing of checks and balances to have freewheeling discussions," he said. "This is a reflection of the notion that universities are no longer centres of inquiry and learning, but they are businesses and students are customers. Big business – funders, donors and corporations – is dictating a lot of what universities do in

terms of research and there is also politically motivated pressure in that regard."

Lack of open discussion is also an issue for the student population, agrees Snyder, saying there is a "worrying trend from both left and right to silence and punish political views you don't agree with".

But does this lack of open debate open the door for authoritarian leaders and autocrats to take over? Levitsky has concerns. "We're in a crisis, but we're not that close to an authoritarian regime because we have a strong, robust opposition," he said.

But he believes that the dysfunction and abusive politics may lead people to lose faith. "If that happens they are more likely to vote for demagogic alternatives who offer simple solutions. The next demagogue may be more intelligent and politically astute than Trump."

And while Snyder agrees that such a takeover is some way off, he does sound a warning.

"When conversation becomes so accusatory, people turn off their brains and we run the risk of bringing someone into power who makes it difficult for a democracy to function properly. People need to have access to good information and be able to address issues – both elected officials and voters need those skills.

"The ultimate goal is to have a government that addresses real social problems. To study these problems we have to see them from various angles, with both parties working together to solve them, but we no longer do that at the federal level," he added. "We have political parties who have walled themselves off and homogenous communities electing people who aren't going to bring us together." ⊗

Jan Fox is the US contributing editor for Index on Censorship. She is based in Los Angeles

The party is the law

With hundreds of lawyers in prison, it is hard to challenge the state, says **Karoline Kan**

48(02): 23/25 I DOI: 10.1177/0306422019858481

"**WE CAN HAVE** no hair, but you can't have no law," shouted four women who had gathered in the central park of a Beijing residential compound and were taking turns shaving each other's heads. In Mandarin, "no hair" and "no law" are homophones.

In front of neighbours, foreign journalists and secret plain-clothes police, the women put their hair in a transparent plastic box along with pictures of them and their husbands. This all took place in December last year.

The women are wives of four of China's most prominent human-rights lawyers, who have been arrested and jailed since the "709 crackdown" in which about 300 lawyers and activists were detained throughout China. The purge, which started on 9 July 2015, targeted lawyers who defended political dissidents, victims of illegal land seizures and people who were jailed for practising religion without the state's approval. When they were found guilty, their crimes were stated as being "subverting state power".

A few weeks later, when lawyer Wang Quanzhang was sentenced to four and a half years in jail, his wife Li Wenzu, one of those who shaved their heads, tweeted: "Wang Quanzhang is not guilty, the public prosecution law is guilty!"

Since the day her husband was detained, Li has been on a long, hard journey of constant petitions to the supreme judicial court, meeting international media and calling for leniency and justice. However, no one with any power in China will speak out to help her, and there is little hope that the verdict on her husband will change. This is a country where executive, judicial and legislative powers are all under the control of the Chinese Communist Party, which sees activism and defending political reform, human rights, and separation of the three powers as threats to social stability and its rule.

Although China's constitution says that the People's Court has the right to adjudicate independently, it also formally says the CCP's leadership is the "most essential characteristic" of China's current political system, which means the party is above the constitution.

In Chinese law, there isn't any punishment for CCP officials interfering in judicial work. Besides, local governments and CCP committees control the personal and financial arrangements of the local courts, so it's impossible for Chinese courts to be independent.

CCP organisations even decide some "major and complex" cases, such as those which involve ethnic relationships, religion and political dissidents.

There has been a wave of calls for changes to the judiciary since China's economic reform (known in China as "Reform and Opening Up"). As the country invited foreign business and embraced the development of the private economy, it needed more educated and →

The women are wives of four of China's most prominent human-rights lawyers, who have been arrested and jailed since the "709 crackdown" in which about 300 lawyers and activists were detained throughout China

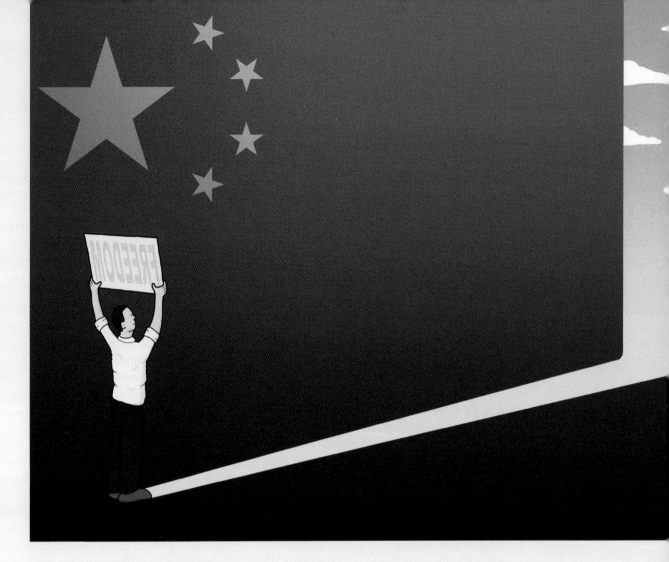

CREDIT: Tjeerd Royaards/Cartoon Movement

→ professional people in the judicial sector as the reforms created more business disputes.

What's more, as China opened up to the West, Chinese legal professionals called for a separation of the judiciary from the control of the administration.

"At that time [the 2000s and early 2010s], many Chinese law experts openly talked about the importance of judiciary reform, and the supreme judicial court even organised meetings for drafting reform proposals," said law scholar and writer Zhao Guojun.

People have gained more freedom and rights compared with the time before Reform and Opening Up. The government has given more independence to courts dealing with soft cases, such as those about environmental and business issues, and tried to make some attempts to make the judicial procedure more transparent, including live-streaming some trials.

However, once the reformers tried to touch the core problems – issues regarding organs of state power violating human rights, freedom of speech, and high-ranking party officials' corruption – the reform could not continue.

It worsened after President Xi Jinping took power in 2013. Xi openly stressed the importance of the party's leadership over China's legal system. He wrote in an article published in Qiushi Journal, a periodical belonging to the CCP: "We must never follow the path of constitutionalism, the separation of powers or the judicial independence of the Western world."

Meanwhile, officials in the judicial system are busy showing their loyalty to the party to avoid being purged. In January 2017, China's chief justice, Zhou Qiang, denounced the idea of an independent judiciary and other liberal principles in a speech to a group of legal officials. "We should resolutely resist erroneous influence from the West: 'constitutional democracy', 'separation of powers' and 'independence of the judiciary'," he said.

He Weifang, a law professor at Peking University, wrote in his blog: "This is truly a statement that wrecks the nation and harms the people. It truly goes against history." The blog was later deleted. "Years ago, when we talked about reform, we used 'judicial neutrality' instead of 'judicial independence' most of the time, because the latter is more sensitive. But today even 'judicial neutrality' is rarely heard," added Zhao.

The result is that China's judicial system has less and less power to resist interference from party officials, especially in cases where the latter's economic interests or the state security apparatus are involved. Thoughts and words that the party doesn't like become crimes, and the courts can do nothing to bring justice.

Nobel Peace Prize laureate Liu Xiaobo was sentenced for "subversion of state power" because he drafted Charter 08, which called for a new constitution guaranteeing human rights, the election of public officials and freedom of religion and expression. In 2018, Tibetan activist Tashi Wangchuk was sentenced to five years for "inciting separatism" because of an interview with The New York Times in which he expressed his worries about losing his language and culture.

In 2015, after a year and seven months in detention, lawyer Pu Zhiqiang was given a three-year suspended jail sentence for "inciting ethnic hatred" and "picking quarrels" in social media posts. One of the posts presented to the court as evidence said: "Why wouldn't China work without the Communist Party? How would I know why it wouldn't work? Other than fraud, evasion, axes and sickles, what's this party's secret for staying in power?"

What's worse is that Chinese media is controlled by the party and the government, and on sensitive and important cases media coverage is heavily censored to influence public opinion.

In December 2018, for example, Wang Quanzhang's trial was conducted behind closed doors, with journalists and foreign diplomats barred from entering the courthouse. There wasn't any in-depth coverage of the case in China other than by a few outlets which reposted the government's official announcement.

"When the ruling party has the absolute power, it will create a monopoly and verbal hegemony, and its power will filter into any aspect of the society, including public speech," said Zhao. "Journalists, professors and artists should speak and act – that's the nature of their roles."

He added that nowadays people such as these dared not talk as even private conversations could be used as evidence of a crime.

The crackdown on civil society and the tightening control of the media are creating a vicious circle in China. When civil society is attacked, the media can't make their voices heard; and when the media find themselves dancing on an iron chain, nobody in civil society can go to the street to speak for them.

Li has not been allowed to meet her husband in more than three years. When she took part in a protest march demanding an explanation for his arrest earlier this year, the authorities stopped the march and placed her under house arrest. But no Chinese media ever reported these stories. It was as if she and her family did not exist. Meanwhile, Zhao's account on Wechat, China's most popular social network app, was suspended for a few days with the reason given that it was "spreading fake information". Zhao doesn't know which information was problematic but he is sure it must be something related to politics.

Zhao chooses to believe in a better future. He said: "Of course, what is in front of us now is sad. Judicial reform and independence is not allowed to be discussed, and everyone is showing their political loyalty. However, I believe technology will help to create a space for people to express [themselves]. Although currently there is fear, fear [will] not rule the future forever." ⊗

Karoline Kan is a Beijing-based writer and journalist and author of Under Red Skies published by Hachette

Balls in the air

The democratic future of Brazil looks shaky.
Conor Foley examines President Jair Bolsonaro's
threats, use of patronage and whether the legal
establishment is too close to power

48(02): 26/28 | DOI: 10.1177/0306422019858496

BRAZILIAN SOCIETY HAS probably never
been more deeply polarised since its return
to democracy in the 1980s. Its new president,
the far-right Jair Bolsonaro, who assumed
office at the start of this year, was elected on a
"tough on crime, tough on corruption" ticket,
appealing to many Brazilians who felt that the
previous Workers Party (PT) governments had
been weak on both.

During the presidential election campaign,
Bolsonaro refused to participate in debates,
hold press conferences or conduct interviews
with journalists where he would have to
respond to questions. He relied instead on
Twitter and other social media to build a huge
network of supporters, including three powerful conservative lobbies: evangelical Christians,
agribusiness and the gun lobby (sometimes
known as the Bible, Bull and Bullet Benches).
His political base in Rio de Janeiro links him
to a feared group of militias who are suspected
in the involvement of the torture and killing of
journalists and opposition politicians. During
the election, he repeatedly attacked both the
media and the judiciary, who he complained
were conspiring against him, and stated that he
would not accept the result if he lost.

According to Human Rights Watch, more
than 140 reporters covering the elections were
harassed, threatened and, in some cases, physi-
cally attacked. Meanwhile, some critics of the
direction in which Brazilian society is moving
have received death threats and have already
left the country. Since the election, Bolsonaro
has continued to rely mainly on social media,
consciously modelling the tactics of US President
Donald Trump. While the US media is a
robustly defended institution in a stable
democracy, however, freedom of expression
in Brazil rests on much shakier foundations.

As Dilma Rousseff, its former president,
noted in her contribution to my new book,
In Spite of You: Bolsonaro and the New
Brazilian Resistance: "Since the universal
vote and direct elections were adopted in
Brazil, in 1946, only five presidents of the
republic have been able to conclude their
mandates. More often than not we have
lived in states of constitutional exception."

Indeed, to understand the rise of Bolsonaro and why he represents such a threat to
democracy in Brazil, it is necessary to explain
a little bit of background about how Rousseff
was ousted from the presidency.

Bolsonaro's election was a by-product of
a corruption investigation – the Lava Jato
(Operation Car Wash), which began in 2013. A
group of judges led by Sérgio Moro devised a
prosecution strategy which was to be the biggest
in Brazilian history, netting the heads of leading
companies and senior politicians. By the end of
2017, more than 300 people had been charged
and more than 1,000 warrants issued.

The effect on public opinion was electric.

Sérgio Costa is a professor at the Institute
for Latin American Studies at the Freie Univer-
sität in Berlin. He is also a contributor to In
Spite of You, where he noted: "Between 2003
and 2013, Brazil's GDP grew 64%, poverty
halved, the minimum wage increased by 75%
in real terms and millions of new formal jobs
were created every year.

"Since 2014, however, Brazil has faced a political and economic crisis generating recession,

*During the election, he
repeatedly attacked both
the media and the judiciary,
who he complained were
conspiring against him*

CREDIT: Paulo Whitaker/Reuters

lower formal employment and higher household debt. GDP annual growth rate fell from 7.6% in 2010 to 0.1% in 2014 and contracted by 3.5% in 2015 and 3.6% in 2016."

The narrative that the economic crisis was caused by politicians looting the public finances was a compelling one, although one with little factual basis. Lava Jato probably actually deepened the crisis through its chilling effect on business confidence.

The measures used by the Lava Jato investigators were certainly controversial. Suspects were placed in pre-trial detention in Brazil's notoriously overcrowded prisons and were offered plea-bargains as inducements to testify. Evidence gathered in this way was used to target more suspects, and the unsubstantiated word of alleged accomplices has been deemed sufficient for conviction. Brazil has a civil law system in which judges have an investigative as well as an adjudicative function. This means that judges sitting without juries have overall direction of a criminal investigation and then determine the guilt or innocence of the defendant.

Many also saw a blatantly political agenda behind the investigations. As Eugenio Aragão, a former minister of justice – previously a public prosecutor – said: "Lava Jato was an entirely political process with a clear political aim: [to] bring down a democratically-elected president and install a more market-friendly replacement."

Politicians from all parties were charged, but public outrage focused on the governing left-of-centre PT. Rousseff, one of the few leading politicians untouched by allegations of personal corruption, was impeached in 2016. Many

ABOVE: Brazil's President Jair Bolsonaro attends a military service in Resende, Brazil, December 2018

of the Congress members who voted for her impeachment were themselves under investigation in the Lava Jato.

Moro provided the Brazilian media with selective briefings about the evidence facing key defendants and tipped them off about police raids so that these could be televised. He also leaked a wiretapped conversation between former President Luiz Inácio Lula da Silva (known as Lula) and Rousseff, while the latter was in power, to the media, significantly contributing to the campaign for her impeachment.

Lula had announced plans to stand in the presidential elections of October 2018 and all opinion polls showed that he would have →

those from the poorer states of the north-east; and he has said that the dictatorship's only mistake was that it did not kill enough of its political opponents.

When casting his vote for the impeachment of Rousseff in 2016, Bolsonaro dedicated it to the memory of the head of intelligence of the military dictatorship responsible for torturing more than 100 political dissidents, including Rousseff herself. On the eve of his election, he released a statement in which he promised to imprison his political opponents and echoed a slogan from the dictatorship era: "Brazil: love it or leave it".

Bolsonaro's inauguration speech on 1 January 2019 vowed to liberate Brazil from "socialism, gender ideology, political correctness and ideology that defends bandits". Unfurling the Brazilian flag, he declared that it would "never be red unless our blood is needed to keep it yellow and green". Hours after taking office, he announced a new regulation transferring the protection and regulation of indigenous land rights to the ministry of agriculture, which is now dominated by the country's powerful agribusiness lobby. Perhaps most significantly, the very first ministerial appointment made was of Moro as the head of a new super-ministry of justice and security. The judge who had presided over the process that had brought down one president and led to the imprisonment of another had become the first beneficiary of the political patronage of a third. These are dangerous times to be a democrat in Brazil. ⊗

Bolsonaro dedicated it to the memory of the head of intelligence of the military dictatorship responsible for torturing more than 100 political dissidents

→   won it quite easily. However, criminal charges were brought against him by Moro and he was imprisoned in April 2018 after a trial which raised many legal concerns. It was Lula's removal from the race that proved the vital fillip to the far-right Bolsonaro, a previously marginal candidate. Bolsonaro is a former military officer and an outspoken supporter of the previous dictatorship. His notoriety comes from a series of bizarrely offensive statements that he has made during his career. He told a fellow legislator that she was too ugly for him to rape her; he said that he would rather his son died than accept him as gay; he has repeatedly taunted Afro-Brazilians, indigenous communities and

Conor Foley *is a visiting professor at Pontifícia Universidade Católica do Rio de Janeiro and editor of* In Spite of You: Bolsonaro and the New Brazilian Resistance, *(OR Books, June 2019)*

Power and glory

While the importance of the Catholic church is waning in most of Europe, it still exercises huge influence in Spain. **Silvia Nortes** finds out why

48(02): 29/31 I DOI: 10.1177/0306422019858503

THE EXCESSIVE AND ongoing power of the Catholic church is a hot topic in Spain. It is the subject of an acclaimed new book by investigative journalist Ángel Munárriz and also of a recent report by the think-tank, Ferrer i Guàrdia Foundation.

According to the foundation, only 26.6% of the population go to church. But the church still wields huge influence over key aspects of Spanish society and enjoys enormous privilege, despite this fall in the number of practising Catholics.

Juanjo Picó, from Europa Laica, an association working towards "protecting the state from any religious interference", goes further. He says that as Spanish society has become less religious, the power of the church has become surprisingly large.

"Society is secularised," he said. "But, in the institutional field, the intrusion of the church has grown since the beginning of democracy."

Munárriz's book, Iglesia S.A. concentrates on the money and power of the church in major areas of Spanish society. The elites of the Catholic church in Spain, he told Index, are historically intertwined with the state. And he argues that successive governments have not addressed the full separation of church and state. Today, this relationship underpins the economy and education, and the church still has influence in areas such as the judiciary.

The omnipresence of the modern church is based on the 1979 agreement between the Spanish state and the Holy See. After the end of Franco's dictatorship, the new constitution established the non-denominational nature of Spain. Even so, the clergy maintained its privileges, which were mainly economic.

Article II of the agreement established the commitment of the state to "collaborate with the Catholic church in the attainment of its economic sustainability".

"A young, non-denominational democracy assuming its duty to economically co-operate with an institution that sustains a particular creed borders on unconstitutionality", said Munárriz.

The church is sustained mainly through taxes. Each year, Spaniards can mark the so-called "church box" on their income statement to allocate 0.7% of their contributions to the church. Fewer and fewer are doing it. Only 14.2% of taxpayers, according to the Ferrer i Guàrdia Foundation, actively decide to contribute taxes to the church, but the total amount the church receives is extracted from the money collected from all taxpayers. As Munárriz puts it: "Catholics decide that we all pay to finance the church."

There is also indirect financing, according to Picó, who was referring to tax privileges such as the exemption from paying the IBI – the real-estate tax – on buildings of religious worship. In the absence of national data, Europa Laica estimates the church is exempt from paying almost $800 million per year.

In its defence, the church points out that mosques or synagogues do not pay, either, and neither do charities. Munárriz takes issue with this. "The church is the largest real-estate owner in Spain. Its exemptions have an incomparably higher incidence," he said.

Its non-profit nature is also in question. "Visitors have to buy tickets in at least 40 out of 78 Spanish cathedrals, [as well as at] dozens of churches, basilicas, monasteries and museums."

He also says education is essential to perpetuate the church's social influence. →

The church still has influence in ... the judiciary

RIGHT: Believers gather before a statue of Jesus during the Semana Santa (Holy Week) procession on 19 April 2019 in Hospitalet de Llobregat, Spain

→ The system for public financing of private schools was launched in 1985. Since then, no government has worked for the end of the so-called educational accords.

Moreover, according to the ministry of education, Spain devoted more than $6.8 billion to private education in 2017 – $184 million more than in 2009. But as Munárriz explains, 2016 investment in public education was still $7.2 billion less than in 2009, and most of the private schools which receive public funds are church-owned.

In 2013, the Organic Law for Improving the Quality of Education (LOMCE), approved by the conservative People's Party government, required schools to offer the Catholic religion as a subject, with bishoprics deciding the curriculum and textbooks.

In Resurrección Galera's case, the church thought it could stop her teaching because of the way she ran her private life. She had been teaching Catholicism in Almería's Ferrer Guardia public school for seven years when, in 2001, she married a man who had been divorced.

As a result, Almería's Bishopric decided not to renew her contract. She took it to the supreme court and last year was reinstated. The court had declared the dismissal was void "for violation of fundamental rights".

Galera's case shows the church's power when hiring and firing teachers. But it is the state that pays their salaries. According to online newspaper eldiario.es, the ministry of education has spent an average of $112 million each year on religious education teachers during the past nine years. "Public money is being devoted to indoctrinate," concluded Picó.

The shadow of the church also falls on the judicial system. "Spanish justice is secular and non-denominational," said Munárriz. "But the presence of Opus Dei in the judiciary is important." Opus Dei is a Spanish institution of the Catholic church that manages universities, schools and hospitals and places its members in the highest levels of the state.

For instance, constitutional court magistrate Andrés Ollero is a well-known opponent of abortion. In 2018, he voted in favour of the constitutional court sentence that concluded segregated private schools were allowed to receive public subsidies.

There are 109 segregated schools receiving Spain's public money. According to Munárriz, 62 of these centres have direct links with Opus Dei. "We consider it normal for an Opus Dei member to vote on abortion or segregated education from the constitutional court ... what if [the court] had a communist magistrate?"

The presence of the church in the judiciary also raises concerns on free expression. "Freedom of expression in Spain is clearly limited when it comes to talking about the church," said Picó. Spain is one of 71 countries that include the offence "to the feelings of the members of a religious confession" in its penal code.

"It is archaic, but the judicial power prevents many legal advances. Why, then, is euthanasia not approved? Why are Catholic schools being state-funded? The judiciary is packed with confessional sects," he said.

In recent months, the Spanish Association of Christian Lawyers has filed lawsuits against theatre companies, artists and actors under

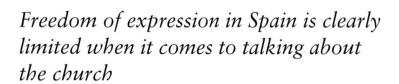

Freedom of expression in Spain is clearly limited when it comes to talking about the church

the guise of "the defence of religious freedom and of all citizens who see their rights are being violated because of their faith". Many complaints are accepted by the prosecution and taken to court. "They want allegations to be registered so that it seems there is a religious persecution going on," added Picó. The Association of Christian Lawyers has even launched an academy to educate "judges and prosecutors who share Christian values".

Munárriz does not think the church is a threat to freedom of expression. "The church in Spain is not just one. There are around 40,000 institutions and each one acts independently. Groups like the Association of Christian Lawyers are more radical, but they go free."

Owning media outlets such as COPE radio station and Trece TV channel makes it easier for them to transmit their message without the need to "attack" others. "The church does not want to be talked about as a repressor. Yes, they polarise debates and generate division, but they do not pursue freedom of expression or press," he concluded.

Picó is adamant, though, that it is time for radical change in Spain, saying: "We must repeal the 1979 agreements with the Holy See." ⊗

Silvia Nortes is a freelance journalist, based in Murcia, Spain

Rowson

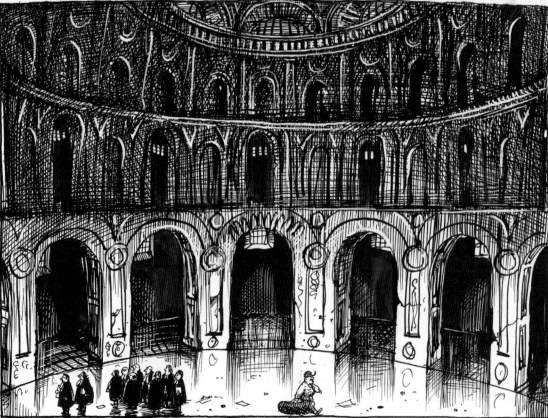

48(02): 32/33 | DOI: 10.1177/0306422019858504

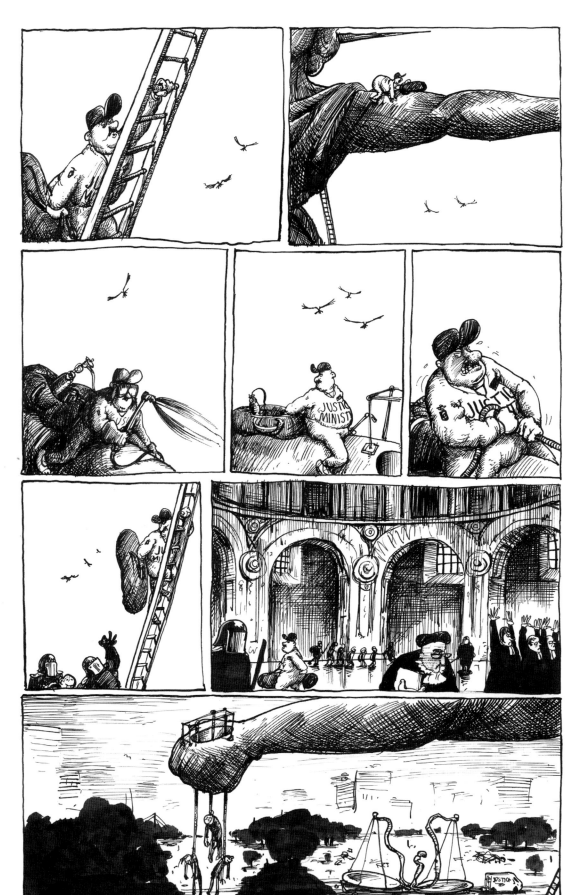

MARTIN ROWSON
is a cartoonist for
The Guardian and
the author of various
books, including
The Communist
Manifesto (2018), a
graphic novel adap-
tion of the famous
19th century book

What next for Viktor Orbán's Hungary?

How Hungary's prime minister has moved to take control of the media and the judiciary. **Viktória Serdült** investigates

48(02): 34/37 | DOI: 10.1177/0306422019858515

ON AN UNUSUALLY warm evening, a poster appeared on the corner of a small street in the Hungarian capital. Tied to a traffic sign, and signed by the government party Fidesz-KDNP, its message was clear: "Send word to Brussels: migration must be stopped". The next morning, however, the poster was gone: only the rope used to tie it remained.

A few blocks away, opposite the beautiful Moorish building of the largest synagogue in Europe, the same poster is sprayed with the letters "O1G", the obscene slogan of the December protests. The abbreviation is short for *Orbán egy geci*, a pithy phrase deriding the prime minister using a Hungarian expletive that literally means "sperm", but is used as a catch-all insult.

But apart from the occasional graffiti, the picturesque streets of Budapest show no signs of the tensions that lie underneath the "illiberal democracy" of Prime Minister Viktor Orbán – seen by some as the saviour of Europe

and by others as an Erdogan-like dictator. The truth is, in Hungary, real changes happen deep below the surface. Watchdogs set the alarm bells ringing long ago, yet Orbán was elected prime minister last year for the third consecutive time. And with the help of his super-majority in parliament, the only question is: how far is he willing to go?

Some would argue he has already gone way too far. When Orbán was not re-elected in 2002, he quickly blamed "left-wing and liberal journalists" for his downfall. His big mistake, he told his biographer at the time, was that he had insufficiently influenced the media. But after coming back to power in 2010, it was not only the media he started transforming: he has spent the last eight years cementing his power, including meddling with the electoral system, getting a super-majority in parliament and taking over the courts.

The biggest blow came last year, when parliament passed a new law allowing the creation of administrative courts that will take over government cases such as taxation and elections from the main legal system. But after months of criticism about political interference in the court system the government announced a U-turn at the end of May. Analysts suggested this was related to pressure from the European People's Party, its grouping in the European Parliament.

The prime minister, who never gives interviews to the independent press, gave a rare insight into his mind when recently speaking to French philosopher Bernard-Henri Levy. Asked why he moved his offices from parliament to a more austere site in the Budapest Castle district, Orbán answered: "Because my old offices were in the parliament building down

Watchdogs argue that centralisation of the judiciary, the press, parliament and the electoral system will have long-term effects on the country

the hill, on the other side of the Danube, and that wasn't good from the point of view of the separation of powers."

But Hungarian and international watch-dogs argue that centralisation of the judiciary, the press, parliament and the electoral system will have long-term effects on the country, from which there will be no return to the path of democracy.

András Kádár, co-chair of the Hungarian Helsinki Committee, is not optimistic. The human rights organisation – whose other co-chair, Márta Pardavi, has just been awarded the Civil Rights Defender of the Year Award by the group Civil Rights Defenders – has been under constant government attack for years. In fact, what Kádár sees is a systematic and parallel deconstruction of critical voices by the Orbán government in every relevant field, from the media to academic independence.

"It always starts with a rhetorical attack," said Kádár, who remembers exactly how, back in 2013, the Hungarian Helsinki Committee started noticing something was wrong. It was when the spokesman of Fidesz used the phrase "foreign-funded activists" for the first time. →

ABOVE: A crowd listens to Viktor Orbán speaking in Budapest, Hungary, in October 2013

→ What they didn't know was that it was only the beginning: the next summer, Hungarian government agents raided the offices of three non-governmental organisations that helped distribute Norwegian grants in the country.

A few months later, Orbán used the phrase "illiberal democracy" for the first time at a youth gathering in Transylvania.

Kádár thinks that such rhetoric has only one goal: to undermine the credibility of anyone who dares to criticise the government.

"Being an NGO, our job is to call attention to misgivings, regardless of any government. By undermining our credibility, they are taking away our most important asset," he told Index.

But the attacks don't stop there. The rhetorical phase is usually followed by a second: an attack on financing, made possible with laws implemented by the parliamentary super-majority. In 2017, a new measure was introduced, requiring NGOs to declare themselves "foreign funded organisations" if they received yearly donations above $24,500.

A year later a law, nicknamed Stop Soros, was introduced making the helping of illegal migration a criminal offence.

The final and decisive battle comes with the third stage, when authorities end co-operation with organisations, making their work extremely difficult. "We don't do our jobs for our own sake, we do it to create a country where basic human rights are respected. But when our credibility is questioned, receiving aid is made almost impossible and authorities stop co-operation, it is not only our clients but the whole society that suffers," said Kádár.

It is not only civil organisations that have experienced these three stages of deconstruction:

Foreign constraints from the EU and US institutions continue to be the major disincentive for national political elites in new democracies to pursue evermore privileged positions

many feel the strain of having to comply with the will of the government.

Take the Hungarian media, for example. Today, there are more than 450 outlets channelled into one giant Central European Press and Media Foundation, all controlled by the government. On the other hand, independent newspapers – those not taken over or shut down – are struggling to make ends meet.

Journalists are not persecuted or imprisoned and they can write what they want, but the core of the problem is "media capture". Media outlets in Hungary are largely driven by state-owned advertising revenues, but since 2010, critical papers have barely had any advertisements from the government. According to the official statistics of the Hungarian media institute Mérték, the independent HVG magazine has not had a single one since December 2014. Many publications have resorted to cutting costs or asking for funding from readers, but a lack of co-operation from the authorities risks creating the perception that these titles lack credibility. "The most important asset of the government is obstructing the work of independent journalists," said Ágnes Urbán, a university lecturer and expert at Mérték.

"Government politicians don't give interviews to independent journalists who could ask them real questions," she told Index. "They don't invite them to press conferences and other important events. Some outlets were even banned from parliament."

As for Orbán himself, it is no secret that after completing his work at home he wishes to play a central role in European politics. Many commentators are already worried that the "system of national co-operation", as he likes to call it, will echo around other countries in the region.

But adopting the Hungarian model requires more than willpower, says Veronica Anghel, a political scientist at SAIS, Johns Hopkins University.

"Viktor Orbán is an original personality in the post-communist central-eastern European setting," she told Index. "It took decades for him to build his dominating position in Hungarian politics, business and media and only then transform the legal-liberal order. This

CREDIT: Mike Flugennock/Cartoon Movement

achievement is still not matched by an equal in the region. But the institutional weaknesses that countries like Romania, Bulgaria and Slovakia are met with are similar."

But what these countries don't take into consideration is the power of the European Union and the USA.

"Complete state capture requires the legal modification of democratic institutions to subvert elite accountability. Foreign constraints from the EU and US institutions continue to be the major disincentive for national political elites in new democracies to pursue evermore privileged positions through this type of alterations," she said.

As for Hungary, the future is still uncertain – but many think Orbán is far from satisfied. At his inauguration speech last year, he said he planned to remain in power until 2030. Seeing what he has achieved in the past, the next 11 years may cause even bigger surprises. One of the next big steps might be waging a war on a completely new front: culture. A new director has already been appointed to lead the main cultural institute of the country, the Petőfi Literary Museum.

Szilárd Demeter plans to make the museum "a power centre of national significance" that would not shy away from politics. His proposed projects include the training of cultural journalists and making it obligatory for artists with government scholarships to take part in its programmes.

Orbán has also started dismantling one of the most prestigious institutions, the Hungarian Academy of Sciences. The academy has always been funded by the government but has retained self-management with the help of a network of scientific research bodies. The recent plan is to separate the networks and

www.sinkers.org

THE NEW HUNGARIAN FLAG

run a new management body, with members selected by the government.

The fate of another academic institution, the Central European University, is still uncertain. The school has already announced its move to Vienna, and although the Bavarian government has recently intervened, there is little chance that the prestigious institute will remain in Budapest. And with the European parliamentary elections looming, many fear that Orbán will break ties with the European People's Party, the only political group that was able to exert some sort of control over the Hungarian leader.

At the moment, experts agree that the best playing cards the Hungarian government hold are uncertainty and surprise. As Kádár says: "The situation is totally unpredictable; you never know what is going to happen next. It might be a new law or the recalling of an old one. And this uncertainty and frustration is what makes our job so difficult." ⊗

Viktória Serdült is a journalist based in Hungary

When justice goes rogue

The rule of law has completely broken down in Venezuela and it is left to journalists to provide "little sparks of light" in the darkness. **Melanio Escobar** and **Stefano Pozzebon** report

48(02): 38/43 | DOI: 10.1177/0306422019858518

VENEZUELA IS OFFICIALLY the worst country in the world for the abuse of judicial power.

The 2019 World Justice Project's Rule of Law Index ranks the country lowest of all the 126 countries listed, and it falls down in every single category – from failing to provide judicial constraints on government powers to fairness in the criminal justice system.

In May this year, the total breakdown of judicial independence led to judges from the supreme court siding with President Nicolás Maduro in accusing 14 members of the opposition party of treason. Three of them feared enough for their lives to take refuge in foreign embassies and Edgar Zambrano, national assembly president Juan Guaidó's deputy,was arrested.

Not only has the supreme court removed parliamentary privilege and immunity from opposition MPs but, with the support of Maduro and the court, security forces have been stationed in front of the national assembly building to intimidate all parliamentarians.

One of the assembly members who has been accused of treason, but has not fled, is Miguel Pizarro. He is an ex-journalist and one of the youngest deputies of the national assembly.

In an interview with Index he said: "The ultimate goal is complete control: political control, social control, control of the economy."

The judiciary has always been weak in Venezuela, a country which regularly comes low down the WJP's index. According to Rodolfo

Montes de Oca, a lawyer for education action programme Provea, one of the oldest human rights organisations in Venezuela, the breakdown of the rule of law started in 2008 with the decision by Hugo Chavez to amend the constitution. This, he said, had been made worse by Maduro, who suspended the rights to a recall referendum; illegally appointed supreme court judges; and suspended the powers

RIGHT: Members of Venezuela's Intelligence Services (SEBIN) detained journalists outside the home of former police commissioner Iván Simonovis, who had earlier escaped from house arrest in Caracas, Venezuela

of the national assembly. This led, from 2017, to arbitrary detentions, military trials for civilians, forced disappearances and the suspension of guarantees and rights. It was made easier because Chavez had systematically weakened all the institutions of government including the military, the judiciary and the supreme court.

In 2016 the opposition polled 14 million votes and took control of the assembly. →

Without any order of detention, SEBIN officials in balaclavas confiscated the journalists' phones and documents

CREDIT: Rafael Briceño Sierralta/NurPhoto/Getty

→ Their victory gave them the power to sack supreme court judges who were loyal to Maduro and even rewrite the constitution.

Maduro's response was to encourage the supreme court to strip the national assembly of its powers and set up a parallel organisation called the Constituent National Assembly, controlled by the judges and Maduro's supporters.

Elections were then called for May 2018.

They were widely thought to be rigged and Maduro won, ending any pretence that there was any separation of powers or that Venezuela had any kind of functioning democracy.

To compound it all, the economy of this oil-rich country is in freefall. Oil exports – which account for almost all the country's export earnings and half of government revenues – have plummeted, exacerbated by falling oil

prices, old infrastructure and, more recently, by US sanctions. US Central Intelligence Agency figures – the only ones available because Venezuela has ceased to collect its own – suggest national deficit stands at 46% of GDP, which is far worse than any other country in the world.

According to a study by the opposition-led national assembly, the annual inflation rate reached 1,300,000% in the 12 months to November 2018. The nation is submerged in total blackout for days at a time because of electricity failures.

When the lights go out, the water also stops because the pumps stop working. People are unable to bathe, to cook, or to flush the toilet properly. This means that ordinary residential buildings begin to stink like the largest sewers in any city. The shops are also closed and it is difficult to get drinking water, medicine and non-perishable food. It feels like being in an apocalyptic scene of some zombie movie.

The only people left to record what is happening are journalists. But journalists are finding it increasingly difficult to operate in the country.

In May, as the crisis deepened, eleven journalists were held for more than four hours in Caracas by the Venezuelan intelligence service SEBIN after filming the home of former police chief Iván Simonovis, who escaped from house arrest in the early hours of the same day. Without any order of detention, SEBIN officials in balaclavas confiscated the journalists' phones and documents. They prevented them from communicating with their newsrooms and relatives, and, after the usual interrogation, let them go unharmed.

Simonovis was convicted in 2002 of killing demonstrators before a failed coup attempt, and widely considered a political prisoner. Guaidó had been calling for his release, so his escape from house arrest was big news for journalists, who had been surpised by the release of another high profile prisoner from house arrest, former mayor Leopoldo Lopez, at the end of April.

The National Union of Press Workers (SNTP) denounced the aggression and urged the immediate release of the journalists.

Foreign journalists have also had problems, according the Committee to Protect Journalists, and are at risk from the authorities and armed groups known as *colectivos*. They have documented brief detentions of journalists and their fixers, journalists threatened at gunpoint. The BBC and CNN reported being censored in the country.

Freedom of the press has long been under siege in Venezuela. According to SNTP's secretary Marco Ruiz, security forces acted against the press on 260 occasions in the first 136 days of 2019, ranging from temporary detention, interrogation without a lawyer, to confiscation of their equipment and deportation.

There is no official freedom of the media. It was controlled long before Maduro stripped the assembly of its power. This control is exercised through The National Telecommunications Commission (Conatel) which is the regime's censoring organisation. It has effectively shut down independent television →

LEFT: Assembly member Biagio Pilieri took a picture on his mobile phone to post on social media after the police prevented him from entering the national assembly in Caracas, Venezuela

The ultimate goal is complete control: political control, social control, control of the economy

It is incredible how the ability of the citizenry to access information and news has deteriorated – it's become a kind of battle ... a game of cat and mouse

→ channels, radio stations, and newspapers and magazines, as well as blocking thousands of webpages and social networks.

Andrés Azupura is the director of Venezuela Inteligente, an NGO in charge of monitoring free expression online. He says the situation for freedom of expression has got much worse as the political and economic situation in Venezuela has deteriorated.

"The past five months have really been the worst for the freedom of the internet," he told Index. "We've seen how, out of 21 important information and news sites in Venezuela, 13 were blocked with the start of the political crisis between Guaidó and Nicolás Maduro. It is incredible how the ability of the citizenry to access information and news has deteriorated – it's become a kind of battle ... a game of cat and mouse."

The economic crisis has also meant that there is not enough money to print newspapers. Panorama, in the western state of Zulia, is the latest daily to announce the end of its print edition after rising costs and regulations on the distribution of paper made it impossible to continue. Many independent journalists are still determined to chronicle this so they can tell the story of how a dictatorial regime decided to hold onto power at any cost in order to perpetuate itself.

Despite the tightening of censorship and the arrests, enterprising journalists have used

HOW DO WE FIND OUT WHAT'S REALLY HAPPENING?

Journalist STEFANO POZZEBON on what it feels like to work as a journalist today in Venezuela

FINDING RELIABLE INFORMATION on what is happening in Venezuela has become a daily battle for journalists, fought through WhatsApp groups, via frantic Twitter scrolls and by using virtual private networks to access blacked-out internet pages too radical to pass the government censors' test.

We are trained to question everything and double-check our sources, but with with few reliable media institutions in which to put their trust, average Venezuelans are also doing that now. "Schools will be closed tomorrow," the rumour spreads. "Who said it? How do we know?"

Both the slums in the outskirts of Caracas and the high-class residential neighbourhoods have become realms of tittle-tattle, where a neighbour's hearsay acquires the same value as a radio bulletin.

"The government will soon announce a new foreign exchange system..."; "There are ongoing talks between the opposition and the government and soon a solution will be found..."

The endless stream of information, true or false, seems only destined to keep flowing.

Venezuela's most famous radio broadcaster, Cesar Miguel Rondon, resigned from his post in February after being told by the government of embattled president Nicolás Maduro how he was to refer to opposition leader Juan Guaidó, and to Maduro himself.

Similar orders are regularly passed on to local TV channels, which operate under the constant threat of being pushed off air if reporters, or guests, do not comply with the government's narrative.

For local reporters, to keep working feels like navigating a minefield – but it's the effect on society as a whole that is more worrisome. Information spreads unconstrained and unchecked to an audience which no longer has the feeling of being informed or even a sense of knowing what is going on.

As the media is pushed out of the public sphere, there are no other institutions capable of playing the same social role, thus leading to a vast gap of misinformation, ignorance and chaos.

Filling the gap – and, by doing so, having informed citizens who are capable of making informed decisions – will be pivotal for the reconstruction of Venezuela and many other countries around the

online resources to continue communicating. By doing so they have exposed themselves to attacks by members of the state and persecution by the political police who punish dissident voices. Azupura said: "On the one hand there are the censors, trying to control everything so that the people don't see certain news items, so they don't hear certain voices; and on the other side are the journalists searching for solutions, innovative ways to reach their audiences. There are also the activists trying to defend the right of people to connect with one another."

An example of one way citizens can be informed and journalists can inform is the independent news website Efecto Cocuyo (The Cocuyo Effect) – an initiative which its own founder, Luz Mely Reyes, categorises as: "small sparks of light".

A *cocuyo* is a small insect which emits light and Reyes says the small snippets of news and social media add up to a bigger light, just like the small sparks do. "All together we can illuminate an entire nation" she said. It is because of this that Pizarro comments that "the citizenry has been left with only two tools in order to communicate: on the one hand the social networks, and on the other protest – but with a deep fear of reprisals and consequences".

It is evident that this total control has affected the ability of Venezuelans to enjoy any freedom of expression. The imposition of the official rhetoric is one of the regime's primary missions now. If they can't control events, at least they can determine how their history is told, without caring that this is achieved by sacrificing the people who once voted for them and placing millions who disagree at risk ⊗

Melanio Escobar is a director of Humano Derecho Radio Estación. Additional reporting by Stefano Pozzebon

world where the media are under siege. Working in Venezuela as a journalist requires a good amount of patience and understanding of your personal limits.

Since blackouts started spreading over the country, communications have become unreliable and travelling is more difficult. As a result, it's often impossible to confirm a fact, check a source or cover an event outside Caracas.

Government officials rarely answer the phones, and even more rarely confirm a piece of information that needs to be sourced.

The supreme court publishes its sentences on a public Facebook page, perhaps because it no longer has IT personnel to maintain a proper institutional website.

In the three years I have been reporting in Venezuela, the growing distance between the story and the storytellers has been one of the biggest obstacles for my profession. It's hard, or often impossible, to get information from one place to another; hard to speak to a first-hand witness; hard to find a reliable colleague to trust.

The little caveat "was unable to independently verify...", which would sound like a surrender to many reporters worldwide, has become the norm here.

The country has effectively had two parliaments since July 2018, and two presidents since January this year, and both camps equally try to spin the narrative in their favour to belittle the opponent.

This almost-total anarchy means that there are no set rules: some police could arrest you just for taking a picture, some won't bother with it. One day a protest gathers tens of thousands of people on the street, and the following day mere hundreds show up. Working as a journalist can be dangerous one time, and absolutely fine the next.

The great Colombian author Gabriel Garcia Marquez and his magical realism created a world where nothing was what it seemed, where X meant Y, and Y meant Z, and where no truth would hold the test of time untouched.

For me, my experience as a foreign correspondent in Venezuela seems very close to that.

Stefano Pozzebon is a freelance reporter and documentary producer. Based in Caracas since 2016, he has worked for CNN, BBC, and VICE News

This almost-total anarchy means that there are no set rules: some police could arrest you just for taking a picture

"If you can keep your head when all about you are losing theirs…"

When it feels as though democracy is crumbling around you, being a journalist can feel very lonely, reports **Caroline Muscat** from Malta

48(02): 44/46 I DOI: 10.1177/0306422019858519

"**RESPECT FOR TRUTH** and for the right of the public to truth is the first duty of the journalist."

This is one of the principles considered as the bedrock of an uncompromising stand in defence of quality and ethical journalism listed in the 1954 Bordeaux Declaration by the International Federation of Journalists.

I defended that truth successfully in the appeal court in Malta this year after a five-year legal battle, during which my work was repeatedly discredited by state-sponsored trolls.

It all started when I was sued for libel in two separate actions by Patrick Dalli, the husband of Equality Minister Helena Dalli, because of articles by me in The Times of Malta about illegal development on a property belonging to a company they both owned. He won the initial action and I was accused of targeting the minister's husband for political purposes and fined €10,000 ($11,260). But in March this year the appeal court overturned the ruling.

I won the case, thanks to the support of The Times of Malta. The newspaper stood by its stories and provided the legal backing. But the state broadcaster worded the news in such as way as to weaken the effect of the result. To this day, an online search on the case results in a string of hits that report the fine, but very little on the appeal victory.

The ruling defended the freedom of the press after the biggest blow ever given to the profession – the assassination of Malta's most prominent journalist, Daphne Caruana Galizia.

"A journalist has a duty to investigate and report on matters of public interest," the appeal judges ruled.

The reaction by the minister's husband was to issue a warning on social media: "Don't worry, Caroline. It's far from over". He proceeded to file a judicial protest, saying his rights had been breached.

There are no repercussions for those in power who threaten journalists in this way. And it is far from the only case. Increasingly, demands are made to remove published stories or face another case in court, no matter how factual the report or the evidence published.

The threat is multiplied by those using a handful of London law firms to threaten journalists with Strategic Lawsuits Against Public Participation (Slapps). These are lawsuits which can financially cripple journalists after taking cases against them in foreign jurisdictions, such as the USA and the UK.

When I launched The Shift News a few weeks after Caruana Galizia's assassination, the first firm to threaten filing a lawsuit against me was

---

To give in to the demand would have meant that The Shift News would have strayed from its mission. What is the point of yet another news portal caving in to power?

Henley & Partners. This is the firm that promotes Malta's controversial and legal cash-for-passports scheme. The letter we received clearly stated in bold, capital letters: "Not for Publication". But it threatened to initiate a Slapp suit unless The Shift News removed a story we had published about the law firm's work in Grenada.

It was impossible to fight it. Lawyers warned me there was no adequate protection. After Caruana Galizia was killed, it emerged that such a Slapp suit had been filed against her in the USA demanding €40 million ($44.8m). This was in addition to more than 40 libel cases she was facing at home.

We thought about the legal tactics used against Caruana Galizia as we were making the decision to fight it. But to give in to the lawyers' demand would have meant The Shift News straying from its mission. And what is the point of yet another news portal which caves in to power?

As I debated possible courses of action with lawyers, we discovered that some mainstream media outlets in Malta had already complied with similar demands by Pilatus Bank to remove stories. The public was not told that the stories had been taken down, even though by doing so the public record was being altered.

Finding lawyers to take on such cases is far from easy. But it has been the one line of defence that has kept The Shift News alive. There are still some lawyers who are prepared to stand with us. They are instrumental in preserving the remnants of our democracy.

So, we refused to comply and we challenged the firm's demand by publishing their letter in full, exposing for the first time how they were operating.

Right now, in Malta, journalists have to spend a disproportionate amount of time fighting back rather than doing their jobs. →

The judiciary plays an essential role in the protection of freedom of expression, press freedom and access to information everywhere

→ Without the lawyers supporting our cases, the legal costs alone would be unsustainable. And the situation is getting worse.

Malta fell 12 places in the Reporters Without Borders' World Press Freedom Index this year. The year before it dropped 18 places. Malta is now ranked 77th out of 180 countries.

The Venice Commission Opinion on Malta states the country does not have separation of powers or constitutional control by the courts, and citizens do not have access to justice in all cases. This was sustained by conclusions of the Council of Europe's anti-corruption body, GRECO, which said Malta's justice system was "at risk of paralysis".

Retired European Court of Human Rights Judge Giovanni Bonello said the function of many of the judiciary was to "rubber-stamp abuse by the powerful" when the courts should be the last wall of defence to protect democracy and the rule of law.

Out of 17 appointments to the judiciary in

Malta under Prime Minister Joseph Muscat, 16 were all relatives of party politicians or connected to the Labour Party in power. "They have started a process that in 50 years' time will still be a problem," Bonello said.

The prime minister steamrolled ahead, appointing another six members to the judiciary. And as this continues, there is hardly any hope left for journalists battling vexatious libel cases intended to silence them, leading to even more self-censorship.

And it is not just a problem for journalists in Malta. The independence of the media and the judiciary have also been described as being under attack in Hungary. The Helsinki Committee reported that laws introduced to restrict judicial independence and the freedom of judges to interpret the law have led to a situation where the government controls the courts. Lack of an independent judiciary means that journalists are left with no legal recourse to defend their work in the public interest.

In Albania, journalists who try to pursue legal recourse often find it difficult to find a lawyer to represent them, particularly when a government member is involved in the case. A report by the US Embassy concluded that the government posed the biggest threat to freedom of expression in that country.

Journalists rarely take action to protect themselves or to seek justice. They resort to self-censorship with the vast majority practising it at some point due to fear of retribution, losing their jobs, threats, or pressure from third-party interference, according to Reporters Without Borders.

The judiciary plays an essential role in the protection of freedom of expression, press freedom and access to information. It ensures the safety of journalists through prevention, protection and by the prosecution of crimes against them, UNESCO stresses. But in parts of Europe right now, this essential element of democracy is being severely eroded. ⊗

BELOW: Journalists protest for freedom of expression, democracy and justice outside the parliament in Valletta, Malta, on 19 October 2017. Threats to Maltese journalists, include rape threats, assaults and assassinations, according to a report by the Mapping Media Freedom project

Caroline Muscat is the co-founder of The Shift News in Malta

CREDIT: Matthew Mirabelli/AFP/Getty

Failing to face up to the past

Twenty-one years after the signing of the Good Friday Agreement – which was supposed to herald a bright and peaceful future – questions abound about Northern Ireland's democratic deficit. **Ryan McChrystal** reports

48(02): 47/49 | DOI: 10.1177/0306422019858520

A FAILURE TO DEAL with a violent past and to expose history to public scrutiny may be linked to why significant numbers of young people in Northern Ireland don't trust their regional government.

"The poison of the past is a toxic influence on the politics of the present, and always will be, unless we can honestly face up to what happened," said journalist Anne Cadwallader, author of Lethal Allies: British Collusion in Ireland, a book using historical documents to show how part of the British army and the Royal Ulster Constabulary worked with extreme loyalist gangs, leading to the killings of around 120 people in counties Armagh and Tyrone in the 1970s.

Loyalists in Northern Ireland want to stay part of the United Kingdom rather than joining with the Republic of Ireland. The term is often used to describe those who are prepared to use, or support, violence.

Cadwallader added: "The battle has now moved from bombs and bullets to conflicting versions of history."

Some 36% of 18-to-30-year-olds surveyed earlier this year said they had no trust in the Northern Ireland Assembly, according to a report from the British Council, while only 2% had "complete trust".

The assembly – set up as part of the 1998 Good Friday Agreement reached by Northern Ireland's politicians and the British and Irish

governments – has been suspended since 2017 after a row between the two main parties over a £490 million overspend of public funds.

Kieran McEvoy, a professor of law and transitional justice at Queen's University Belfast, told Index that the failure to deal with history played no small part in corroding public confidence in political institutions.

One way information about that history is now coming to light is through testimony to public inquests. But these are not always straightforward, and are limited in scope.

When Democratic Unionist Party leader Arlene Foster was first minister, she tried to block a plan to complete inquests into 94 controversial deaths dating back to The Troubles within five years. The High Court ruled in 2018 that she was acting unlawfully, and the decision was overturned.

"Actions like Foster's corrode trust between political parties and make it difficult for republicans to sell to their constituents – who are putting on the pressure around legacy inquests – continued power-sharing with the DUP," McEvoy said.

However, the single biggest frustration to legacy issues is the British government's continuing obfuscation over the role of the →

We lifted a corner of the carpet and they are now trying to nail it down forever

RIGHT: Ciarán MacAirt (centre) from the Time for Truth campaign announces a march in June 2019 to demand funding for further inquests into those killed during the Troubles, a period of conflict in which an estimated 3,700 were killed

TIME FOR TRUTH
March on Sunday 9th June
Assembles at 12.00pm
Divis Tower • Cromac Square • McGurk's Bar Memorial

INDEXONCENSORSHIP.ORG

HIGH COURT RULES ON PRESS FREEDOM IN NORTHERN IRELAND

IIIIIIIIIIIIIIIIIIIIIIIIIIIIIIIIIIIIIIIIIIIIIIIIIIII

INDEX AND ENGLISH PEN intervened in the case of journalists Trevor Birney and Barry McCaffrey, who were arrested and questioned last year following armed raids on their homes. They were arrested over allegations that a confidential document, featured in their documentary No Stone Unturned, had been stolen from the Police Ombudsman of Northern Ireland. This was despite a statement from the ombudsman's office saying no theft had been reported. The investigative documentary examines claims of state collusion in the murders of six men.

During the raid, police seized documents, personal computers and USB sticks belonging to family members and copied a computer server that contained years of sensitive reporting.

The Lord Chief Justice of Northern Ireland Sir Declan Morgan quashed the warrants at a judicial review at the High Court in Belfast and, in early June, ordered the return of materials.

→   state in the conflict, Cadwallader says, with a tactic of "deny, delay and die".

"Deny what happened; when evidence emerges delay proceedings through the courts and so on; and hope that, eventually, those people who lost loved ones during the conflict will just die."

Families – along with journalists, academics and campaigners – have endeavoured over the years to uncover the truth, sometimes with great success. They rarely do this without coming up against the British Official Secrets' Act or being stonewalled by the "security veto", where information is denied on national security grounds, or by finding that important documents have been lost or destroyed in suspicious circumstances.

"It was a pretty dirty war, and a lot of wicked stuff happened in terms of state torture, collusion and all the rest of it, so there are elements of the military and security establishment that are not keen for that past to be exposed," McEvoy told Index. "The British state has done a lot to undermine legacy-related work, and that's been most obviously manifest in the failure to have a public inquiry into the Pat Finucane case."

Pat Finucane was a Belfast solicitor who challenged the British government in the 1980s over human rights issues. His most famous client was the Irish Republican Army hunger-striker Bobby Sands, who achieved international publicity for the republican cause by demanding that he and others should be treated as political prisoners.

But Finucane was murdered by loyalist paramilitaries in 1989, with several subsequent investigations suggesting they were supported by the British security forces.

In 2012, UK Prime Minister David Cameron apologised to his family for the "shocking levels" of British state collusion with loyalist parties in his killing, as revealed in the Pat Finucane Review, headed by barrister Desmond de Silva. And in February 2019, the UK Supreme Court ruled that the investigation into his murder was ineffective and didn't meet human-rights law standards. But despite these findings, no full public inquiry to get to the bottom of the murder has been authorised by the government. Indeed, back in 2011, Cameron reportedly told the Finucane family that "people in buildings all around here," gesturing around Downing Street, "won't let it happen".

Researchers attempting to discover the truth about past actions say they find obstacles in their way. Last year, a record number of historical documents were withheld by the British security forces, including documents relating to Finucane's murder.

Setbacks for affected families have only increased since the Historical Enquiries Team, a unit of the Police Service of Northern Ireland, tasked with investigating unsolved murders, was closed down in 2014 because of budget cuts. Cadwallader says that although the HET was imperfect, she could not have written Lethal Allies without it. "It was a unique experiment that's unlikely to be repeated because what we got was so damning," she said. "We lifted a corner of the carpet and they are now trying to nail it down forever."

Nailing down the carpet was perhaps the intention when the police arrested Belfast journalists Trevor Birney and Barry McCaffrey in August 2018 for their work on No Stone Unturned. The award-winning documentary examined state collusion in the 1994

Loughinisland massacre, when members of the loyalist Ulster Volunteer Force killed six civilians and wounded five others in a pub in County Down. More than 100 officers turned up at the journalists' homes accusing them of document theft, under the UK's Official Secrets Act. Charges were dropped in June.

In order to deal properly with the legacy of Northern Ireland's troubled past, all sides must be more open, Cadwallader adds, and that includes the Irish government and paramilitaries.

On the non-state side, a reluctance to open up "is down to risking political leverage, protecting political careers, and reputational damage", Anthony McIntyre, a former IRA man imprisoned for the murder of a member of the UVF in 1976, told Index.

McIntyre was a lead researcher on an oral history project at Boston College, in the USA, that collected testimonies from former republican and loyalist paramilitaries on the condition that they would only be made public after their deaths. "We were conscious that without the retrieval and preservation of historical material, valuable material would be lost to posterity," he said.

The British government and the Northern Irish police used subpoenas and the US court system in attempts to access the archive, and in October 2018 the UK's High Court ordered that McIntyre's interviews be handed over. He is currently taking an appeal to the UK Supreme Court. He says the actions of the state have "limited understanding of the conflict" and have suffocated the ability of future historians and researchers. "It also puts police in charge of what society will know about major

areas of activity that is deemed illegal."

But McEvoy argues that overall responsibility for legacy lies with the UK parliament at Westminster. "It is not a devolved matter, and even the PSNI want it off their plate," he said.

"I'm also not a zealot in terms of the relationship between truth and reconciliation. The truth will not suddenly reconcile us all, but it does 'narrow the space for permissible lies'," he adds, referencing the words of Canadian historian Michael Ignatieff in this magazine (Articles of Faith, Vol 25, 2/1996, p111).

Without a proper understanding of the history of the conflict by the British public, legacy issues will only get so far, says Cadwallader. "They think they know what went on during the conflict – that it was a war between two atavistic tribes in which the British government was a neutral arbiter – but they can't know because they're not being told."

And without a clearer understanding of their past and a sense that the truth is being told, the people of Northern Ireland will continue to mistrust those who govern them. ⊗

ABOVE: Nichola Corner, sister of murdered journalist Lyra McKee, at the end of a three-day peace walk from Belfast to Derry. Speakers called on politicians to come together to resolve differences and restart the Northern Ireland Assembly

The poison of the past is a toxic influence on the politics of the present, and always will be, unless we can honestly face up to what happened

Ryan McChrystal is assistant web editor at Index on Censorship

GLOBAL VIEW

Small victories do count

International support for individuals living under oppressive regimes is a vital step towards change, argues **Jodie Ginsberg**

48(02): 50/51 I DOI: 10.1177/0306422019857912

EARLIER THIS YEAR, I spoke on a panel about denialism, which is a refusal to accept agreed facts on historical events, such as the Holocaust; or scientific data on climate change. It was a gloomy group. The other panellists saw a dark and dismal future. I was the sole champion for hope.

These are scary times. Supposedly democratic countries look increasingly like authoritarian ones. Far-right extremism is on the rise. The space for civil society is shrinking. That has given organisations such as ours pause for thought. If governments are no longer bending to international moral pressure – especially pressure from other governments – should we abandon some of the old ways of effecting change: joint letters to those in power, petitions, media clamour, protest? Does any of it make a difference?

The answer is, yes. Yes, it does.

In April, Murad Subay, a Yemeni street artist and the 2016 Index on Censorship Freedom of Expression Awards Arts Fellow, made a visa application to study at a French university as part of a one-year grant for threatened artists. It was rejected. Subay, who creates murals protesting against Yemen's civil war, was given a grant to study under a fund that places artists at risk in safe countries where they can continue their work and plan for their future. Such support is vital in ensuring artists can continue to flourish. It gives them much-needed respite,

but also stresses to the artists' host country that they have international support.

Incensed by France's decision, Index issued a statement urging the authorities to change their minds. "A growing number of supposedly democratic countries such as the UK frequently refuse visas to foreign authors, musicians and activists for events or training," I said at the time. "This reinforces the notion that constraining artistic freedom is acceptable."

We emailed the French embassy. Other organisations protested. Two weeks later, France reversed its decision.

We had a similar experience last year when the UK twice refused visas to our 2018 Freedom of Expression Award winners, the Museum of Dissidence. The second time, when the UK refused a visa for the Cuban artists to take up an artistic residency in Southend, we kicked up a fuss, issuing a statement condemning the decision. A few days later, Luis Manuel Otero Alcántara and Yanelys Nuñez Leyva were called to the UK embassy in Havana and told the visas would be granted after all. Their application had been "re-evaluated".

These changes of heart may seem like small victories but they are important. Visa practices send an important message to other states about a country's attitude to human rights and the kinds of individuals they are willing to support. Denying visas to individuals who have faced oppression in their own countries emboldens the oppressors.

Making noise internationally about those targeted by authoritarian regimes can offer protection. In 2012, journalist Idrak Abbasov was brutally attacked while he reported on

The nomination made the government back off. You don't realise it, but you buy people more time with the work you do

the demolition of houses in his village. Just weeks before, he had given a powerful acceptance speech on winning an Index Freedom of Expression Award.

"In Azerbaijan", he said, "telling the truth can cost a journalist their life". He suffered broken and fractured ribs, damage to his internal organs and injuries to his eyes. Abbasov says he believes the international support he received kept him alive. "Without international support, it would have been worse," he said of the attack. "Maybe the... award kept me from getting killed."

Appreciation for receiving support is something we hear often from those facing threats from governments. Zimbabwean activist and pastor Evan Mawarire, repeatedly arrested for his criticism of the government, was nominated for an Index award in 2016. "The nomination made the government back off," he said. "You don't realise it, but you buy people more time with the work you do."

Speaking out can have an impact even on those in prison. UK-based Bahraini activist Ali Mushaima spent more than 45 days on hunger strike outside his country's embassy in London. He was calling for better treatment of his imprisoned father, Hassan Mushaima. Though Hassan remains in prison, Ali believes the protest has helped improve conditions not just for his father but for other prisoners, too.

"I came out here because I fear for my father's life, and I will continue fighting to save his life," Ali said when he announced an end to the hunger strike. "But I feel now as a result of my protest and hunger strike, I have many people helping me do that, and that is why I see my protest as a success – not because it exposed how horrible the Bahraini regime and its allies can be but because it showed me the good in all those who support justice."

Protests and letter-writing are traditional ways of calling out governments. Social media can also play a key role in making the kind of fuss that can bring about change. Take the case of Saudi teenager Rahaf Mohammed al-Qunun, who tweeted her demands for asylum after barricading herself in a Bangkok airport hotel room.

The plight of the 18-year-old, who said she

faced death if she returned to Saudi Arabia, was picked up in real-time by prominent activists such as Mona Eltahawy and quickly escalated into a global public online furore that forced governments and UN agencies into action. She has now been given asylum in Canada. The gloom-mongers would argue that all these examples are of individuals. That they don't make a difference. But I disagree. A journey of 1,000 miles begins with a single step, and effecting major change – whether it is shifting the discourse on violence against women via movements such as anti-FGM or #MeToo, or climate change through the actions of movements such as Extinction Rebellion – begins with the actions of one or two individuals calling for change. Our job is to continue to magnify their voices. ⊗

ABOVE: Yemeni street artist Murad Subay, Index's Freedom of Expression Award Arts Fellow for 2016, paints a mural in Hoxton during his fellowship in London

Jodie Ginsberg is CEO of Index on Censorship

BIER
KABARET :
M LICHTPRUNKSAALE DER PASSAGE

PICTURED: A 1919 poster for a cabaret show in Berlin featuring the actor Senta Söneland. The poster was designed by Josef Steiner

SENTA
SÖNELAND

IN FOCUS

Sending out a message in a bottle

Actor **Neil Pearson** talks about why governments fear books being published and reveals his favourite childhood reads to **Rachael Jolley**

48(02): 54/56 I DOI: 10.1177/0306422019858292

"**BOOKS ARE CONVERSATIONS** with people who can't be there in person. That's true as much in fiction as it is in fact. You debate it as you go through. You ask yourself: 'Is that true? Would I do that?' These things are good and useful things for us to do," said British actor Neil Pearson, as he starts to explain his passion for books.

Pearson, most famous for his roles as the sexist TV boss in the Bridget Jones' films and his role as gambler Dave Charnley in cult TV newsroom drama Drop the Dead Donkey, now combines his theatre and screen work with running a rare books business.

His enthusiasm and belief in the power of books explodes from almost every sentence.

"I've been a reader since I could read," he said. "I've been a collector [since] before I even knew I was doing it." He read books avidly as a child, and early pleasures were found in the pages of Enid Blyton, the Canadian/American adventure writer Willard Price and Arthur Ransome, of Swallows and Amazons fame. It soon becomes clear that adventure stories held great appeal for the young Pearson.

BELOW: Actor Neil Pearson

"It wasn't a retreat from anything, it felt like I was running towards something. Running towards adventures, and people and worlds I didn't know," he said.

Pearson's strongly held beliefs in the power of reading extends to his support and involvement with the charity Book Aid International, which sends books to 25 countries around the world – especially those in Africa – as well as helping to train librarians. In 2017 it sent 938,333 new books around Africa to libraries, schools, refugee camps and hospitals, and helped train 158 librarians.

"It's an issue that is quite close to my heart because books have been close to my heart ever since I knew what books were," he said, adding: "The impulse is explained by wanting people to have the same thrill and the same happiness that reading has given me."

As a bookseller, Pearson stocks a collection of works published in Paris between the two world wars and this, it turns out, is a very particular passion.

Not only does he wax lyrical about their importance but he has also written a book about one particular Manchester-born publisher, Jack Kahane, who worked in Paris and published some of the most controversial novels of the era, many of which were banned in other countries.

In fact, Kahane was only able to publish them in France because of a loophole in the French censorship laws that meant they did not cover books published in English.

"That's why the writing expat community was out there during the wars, Ernest Hemingway and James Joyce, because you could write freely but, more importantly, you could publish freely. Without being published you couldn't speak freely."

This legal loophole, believes Pearson, who clearly has spent many hours studying the history of this period, was there because of an intellectual French guilt about the impact of the trials of two writers in the 19th century.

"There had been two prosecutions in the 19th century of French writers, one was against Charles Baudelaire, for Les Fleurs du Mal, the other was against [Gustave] Flaubert for Madame Bovary."

He says the trials caused some anger in the French press. "They were outraged that their artists were not being allowed to think outside the then societal norms," he said.

"Artists are supposed to imagine worlds beyond the worlds that they actually inhabit and it was a source of shame. They were disappointed in themselves for not defending these leaders of men, and they became less inclined to … use those obscenity laws."

Pearson was inspired to research and write a book about the Obelisk Press, an English language imprint based in Paris in the 1930s and run by Kahane, because he considered him an influential character whose story was not well enough known. "He published his books in English at a time when they could be published nowhere else but France," he said.

"He followed on from Sylvia Beach when she published Ulysses in 1922. He published Lawrence Durrell; Radclyffe Hall's Well of Loneliness when it was banned in the UK; [and] he published an early edition, not the first, of Lady Chatterley's Lover."

Kahane was a "very important figure in the fight to break down, once and for all, the laws governing what you could and couldn't publish". He added that those laws were finally "knocked off their hinges with the amazing Lady Chatterley's Lover trial and, as a coda, the Last Exit to Brooklyn trial".

"Those both happened in the early 1960s, but the fight to get to that point started with Jack Kahane's Obelisk Press," he went on. Many controversial books, including James Hanley's Boy, Lawrence Durrell's The Black Book and titles by Henry James, were published by Obelisk. "This was uncharted territory, so I was drawn to it."

There are people who will kill you for publishing what they don't like, and while that still remains true the fight remains unwon

He exudes admiration for what Kahane achieved, and why it was symbolically important. "The fight always goes on, but it is a question of where the pendulum is. [In] that era you didn't have the ability to publish. That right was won. Now we have a different battle we have to protect that right, we have to protect it from those who would take it from us.

"As the murdered cartoonists of Charlie Hebdo would tell you, were they still alive today, there are people who will kill you for publishing what they don't like, and while that still remains true the fight remains unwon."

As Pearson acknowledges, governments →

ABOVE: A revival of the 1980s' play Rita, Sue and Bob Too at the Royal Court theatre in London which nearly got cancelled-in 2017 for being too controversial

What you present to the public can be thought-provoking, and even controversial, but there is an acceptable controversial and an unacceptable controversial

→ have seen books as threats throughout history. "That's why they ban them."

When the conversation weaves back to the work of Book Aid International and what it does, Pearson says the charity delivers books to places where they are not available for geographic and economic reasons, rather than because of censorship. "We are talking about getting books to people that can teach them a skill, that can help them to live. I can't think of a more important thing to do," he said.

But books are not the only thing on his mind. He is concerned about freedom of thought more generally.

Much of Pearson's career has been as a stage actor, as well as appearing in TV dramas such as Between the Lines, for which he was Bafta-nominated, and more recently the BBC's Waterloo

ABOVE: Novelist Dame Rebecca West in London after appearing at the Old Bailey to defend the publication of Lady Chatterley's Lover on 27 October 1960

Road. He appeared in Joe Orton's Loot in the 1980s, a play which had been subject to cuts insisted on by the Lord Chamberlain when it was first performed.

What does he think about censorship within the theatre today? "I think we are in a phase where people are self-censoring as well. Theatres are self-censoring. What you present to the public can be thought-provoking, and even controversial, but there is an acceptable controversial and an unacceptable controversial.

"I think the Royal Court dodged the bullet slightly when there was a revival of Rita, Sue and Bob Too," he said.

In 2017 London's Royal Court theatre announced that although it had planned to stage a revival of Andrea Dunbar's working-class play set in Bradford, it decided it was no longer right to do so. Accusations of censorship flipped around the mediasphere before the Royal Court, which has had a reputation for staging controversial plays throughout its history, rethought its position and decided it would go ahead with the production.

"But that is where you can get yourself into hot water," said Pearson. "You have to be able to encourage looking at something and creating the ability to discern, to factor in when it was written, what the prevailing climate was, how people thought, how people interacted with each other and distill from that their own experience. Please don't tell me, Royal Court, or anyone else, what I may or may not see. Put it on and let me think."

And he added: "If you are genuinely against censorship, you have to be evenhanded against censorship. If your idea of freedom of speech is only allowing people to say what you already agree with, then Goebbels would have no problem with that definition of speech.

"But we have to be able to continue to think." ⊗

Rachael Jolley is the editor of Index on Censorship

CREDIT: Eddie Worth/AP/Shutterstock

Remnants of war

LEFT: Artist and journalist Zehra Doğan, the Index arts fellow for 2019, had her work E Li Dû Man (Left Behind) on show at Tate Modern, in London, in May as part of the Who Are We? project. It features collected objects from Kurdish cities in Turkey, telling stories of those who were killed, injured or fled during clashes with the Turkish army. Her installation is commissioned by Counterpoint Arts in conjunction with the Open University, English PEN and Index

CREDIT: Sean Gallagher

48(02): 57/57 | DOI: 10.1177/0306422019858293

Six ways to remember Weimar

German author **Regula Venske** takes a sideways look at the myths and merits of the Weimar Republic on the 100th anniversary of its creation

48(02): 58/62 | DOI: 10.1177/0306422019858294

1. Weimar is but a myth. You may think of it as a rather small town in Thuringia, in the eastern part of Germany, housing fewer than 65,000 inhabitants. But for most Germans, Weimar simply stands for the best we could come up with: writers Johann Wolfgang Goethe and Friedrich Schiller, of course. Just Google "Weimar: European Capital of Culture in 1999" and you will get the picture. There they stand, the two titans of German literature, forever doomed to monumental size, shaking hands and representing the German classical era. As the two writers shared only some productive 11 years in Weimar, until Schiller's death in 1805, we have cleverly added the names of Christoph Martin Wieland and Johann Gottfried Herder to the classical period, thus broadening the timespan until Goethe's death in 1832. Who cares if hardly anyone, except scholars and freaks, nowadays reads Wieland, or Herder, any more? Weimar is proud to count "as many as three entries in Unesco's World Heritage List", and this is what tourists come to visit Weimar for. Quite a number manage to indulge only in the World Heritage part of the myth, skipping Buchenwald or leaving it "for next time".

2. Among the top 10 sights to visit in Weimar, the Buchenwald Memorial ranks number five of the city's suggestions, calling it "an important venue to recall the crimes committed during the Nazi period. 500,000 visitors come here every year". Buchenwald, of course, is not a myth. To each one of the about 250,000 people from almost 50 nations who were imprisoned there between 1937 and 1945 – among them many renowned politicians, theologians, artists and writers, such as Léon Blum, Jean Améry, Imre Kertész, Jorge Semprún and Elie Wiesel – the place was damn real. It was an infamous forced labour concentration camp where an estimated 56,000 prisoners lost their lives.

Buchenwald ("beechwood forest") sadly represents the dark counterside of the German classical spirit. The camp was first going to be named Ettersberg concentration camp, referring to the small wooded Ettersberg hillock upon which it was established, previously known for a Baroque castle frequented by Goethe, and where European royals would go hunting. But the Nazis did not want to spoil the Goethe connections for Goethe enthusiasts by choosing the wrong name. Ironically, you will find the remains of a Goethe oak on the site of the Buchenwald memorial symbolising the Weimar-Buchenwald dichotomy in a way no writer could ever invent.

3. How does the Weimar Republic fit in? In 2009, the 90th anniversary of its founding date passed almost unnoticed by the German public. But in regards to the 100th anniversary, things seem to have changed. In 2013, a group of Weimar-based citizens founded the Verein Weimarer Republik (the Weimar Republic Society) with the goal of commemorating the 100th anniversary and providing academic research, public discourse and political education. Soon, with the support of the Federal Ministry of Justice and Consumer Protection, another museum in Weimar will open its doors to house the national memory of the Weimar democracy.

But not only does the Weimar Republic receive more attention now, there also seems to

RIGHT: Police outside a cinema in Berlin's Nollendorfplatz patrolling riots by Nazi goon squads against the showing of the film All Quiet on the Western Front in December 1930. The film was banned a week after it opened

CREDIT:AKg-images/TT News Agency/SVT

be a shift of paradigm in the perspective of how Germans view it.

It used to be that Germans, both East and West, grew up with the notion that the Weimar Republic was doomed from the beginning, and that the Weimar constitution with its presidential democracy made it easy for Adolf Hitler to rise, leading to dictatorship straight away. It may well be that people in other countries, namely the USA, would associate Weimar with the thriving arts and culture, as well as sciences, of the 1920s, recollecting names of the cultural elite that would soon be forced to emigrate and who would contribute to American culture thereafter. In Germany, we would refer to the "Golden Twenties" by using the English words rather than the German equivalent. But we tended not to think of the 1920s as a golden period in Germany. So what has changed? What suddenly makes us →

Brecht commented drily that the censors – from a police point of view – had better understood the message of his film than even his most sympathetic critics had

by some new kind of German nationalism? Could it be that – after having reconstructed the Berlin Palace, viewed by many as a seat of imperial power from a time of militarism and national expansionism, and filling it with ethnological artefacts of often unclear provenance from a colonial past – a new kind of nationalism is now ready to reinterpret and digest even the Weimar Republic? Could it be nationalism that makes us boast of the First German Constitution as "one of the most modern constitutions that existed at the time", having influenced several Latin American states, Japan, and even France? Weren't we great in granting women's suffrage as early as November 1918, and doing away with censorship, as had been demanded by brave democrats since 1849?

→ want to speak not only of failure and lost opportunities but of the chances and merits of the Weimar Republic instead?

4. We are witnessing the erosion of democracy and the dissolution of the middle class as well as the corresponding political or democratic "centre" in several parts of the world, including Europe, right now. Naturally, while we try to find ways to stop this process of erosion, we want to concentrate less on the doom and learn more about past hopes and possibilities that somehow got lost in the cause of the historical process but might teach us a useful lesson now. At least one would hope that it might be this interest in history, along with the wish to do better this time, that makes us want to celebrate 100 years of the first German republic and the first German democracy.

But I wonder. Could it also be that this shift in focus might be fuelled, at least partially,

5. The Weimar constitution guaranteed freedom of the press and freedom of expression to every German. However, Article 118 of the Weimar constitution, which ruled out censorship, allowed for two exceptions: with regard to films and with regard to protecting German youth from pulp fiction (*Schmutz und Schund*, trash and rubbish…), viewing these two media as potentially highly influential and appealing to the masses. Accordingly, in May 1920, the *Lichtspielgesetz* was passed, prohibiting films which might endanger public order and security, hurt religious feelings or degrade the German state's reputation in international relations. In Berlin and Munich, centres of German film production, authorities were established

ABOVE: Johann Wolfgang Goethe and Friedrich Schiller, the greats of German classical literature, both lived in Weimar and their statues still stand outside the German National Theatre

to check, and possibly prohibit, films meeting those criteria.

Thus, films in the Weimar Republic were the only media which had to be passed by the censors prior to presentation. Of course, this meant heated debates all through the decade. Among the most spectacular incidents were the riots by National Socialist goon squads at the opening of All Quiet on the Western Front, based on the novel by Erich Maria Remarque, in December 1930. Due to their constant interruptions and threats to the audience, the performance had to be stopped. A week later the Berlin-based film review board prohibited any further showings of the film in Germany. The reasons given were both that the film was a security risk and that it caused damage to the reputation of the country.

In this, they followed the National Socialist arguments, insinuating that the pacifist message would defame German soldiers and damage the reputation of Germany. It was Goebbels himself who admitted in an article that it had been their strategy to turn the issue into a matter of prestige between the movement and the Prussian administration.

Another controversy arose around the film Kuhle Wampe oder Wem gehört die Welt? (Kuhle Wampe, or Who Owns The World?) based on a script by Bertolt Brecht, in 1932. Even the members of the censorship board were highly divided in their opinions of it. Some claiming the film would incite the working masses to mistrust the state, while others cherished its high quality as a work of art. When Kuhle Wampe was prohibited, Brecht commented drily that the censors – from a police point of view – had better understood the message of his film than even his most sympathetic critics had. Public protests were partially successful, as the film was released in the end, although with specific cuts. →

WEIMAR'S HALL OF FAME

Irmgard Keun: was a significant German novelist during the late Weimar period. In her novels she critiqued the social issues that existed in the early 1930s, which specifically included consumerism, the social injustice of Weimar Berlin's class and gender hierarchy, and the limited role and identity of women in society. In 1933 her novels were confiscated, banned and burned by the Nazis. Although she kept publishing her works after 1935, she was ultimately forced into exile in Belgium, and later the Netherlands, in 1936.

Otto Dix: was one of the leading painters during the era. He won the Iron Cross for serving in World War I as a machine gunner on the eastern and western fronts. After the war his paintings are described as having become more cynical, political, and sombre. When Adolf Hitler took power, Dix lost his teaching job in Dresden, and his most significant works were confiscated. Like most artists, he was forced to join the Nazi government's Reich Chamber of Fine Arts. While a part of this group he was only allowed to paint "inoffensive landscapes". However, he did occasionally create allegorical paintings that criticised Nazi ideals. Alongside his friend and acclaimed artist George Grosz, he "drew attention to the bleaker side of life" through his paintings by depicting prostitution, violence, old age, and death. He survived Nazi rule and continued to produce anti-war paintings.

George Grosz: worked alongside Dix to depict anti-war paintings and critiques of Weimar society. After serving in World War I, he settled in Berlin. The topics that he focused on most included political corruption, militarism, the inequalities of capitalism, the mistreatment of war veterans, urban life, Weimar decadence, and eroticism. He left the country soon after Hitler came to power and his work was seen as blasphemous towards the Nazi regime and either placed in Germany's Degenerate Art Exhibition in Munich, or destroyed. He moved to the USA, where he lived until his death in 1959, teaching art in New York, and continuing to create anti-war paintings.

Erich Maria Remarque: was one of Germany's most famous writers during the era. His work, which conveyed a strong anti-war and anti-fascist message, was condemned by the Nazi regime and burned. His German citizenship was taken away in 1938, and in 1939 he left for Switzerland and then the USA to escape from the Nazi government. His sister, Elfriede Scholz, was targeted by the Nazi regime in 1943 and was executed after being charged with "undermining morale" for stating that she considered the war to be lost. He is most famous for the acclaimed novel, All Quiet on the Western Front (1928), which was turned into an Oscar-winning film.

Summer Dosch

One writer who remained in Germany was Erich Kästner. Standing in the crowd, he was witness to the burning of his own books

→ Protests also accompanied the passing of the law to protect the youth from three-penny trash and rubbish. But let us not overestimate the public. In his essays on *Schmutz und Schund*, published in various newspapers in 1926, Heinrich Mann's voice sounds not only sceptical but somewhat gloomy. He points out that the morals of young people have never been deteriorated by reading, but by life itself – by irresponsible elders exposing children to a life brutalised by war and post-war unemployment, inflation and poverty, and the struggle for existence. But whereas the public in Wilhelmine times, including liberal-spirited conservatives, widely protested the moralistic *Lex Heinze* law of 1892, Mann misses a similar cry of outrage in 1926, saying: "Nobody seems to care much anymore whether literature will be under control ..."

His brother, Thomas, founding member of the literature section of the Prussian Academy of Arts, actively joined in the protest against the law on *Schmutz und Schund*, thus turning away from his formerly conservative, apolitical, attitude. And so did the German PEN centre, based in Berlin. Founded in 1924 by rather conservative writers, many of whom had been ardent nationalists in World War I, German PEN became quite politicised in the second half of the decade, with writers realising that it was impossible to abstain from politics and that John Galsworthy's dictum of "No politics under any circumstances in the PEN" took a political standpoint itself. German PEN published remarkable letters of protest against censorship, be it against the prohibition of All Quiet on the Western Front, or against Carl von Ossietzky's conviction on the basis of an allegation of espionage and his 18-month prison sentence

after publishing an article on the rearmament of the German air force (prohibited by the peace treaty) in his magazine, Weltbühne.

Other famous cases could be cited, such as the debates around Arthur Schnitzler's drama, Reigen; charges of blasphemy against a number of renowned writers, including Carl Einstein, Klabund and Carl Zuckmayer; and the voluntary withdrawal of an advertisement for Kurt Tucholsky and John Heartfield's anti-military publication, Deutschland, Deutschland über Alles by the German Publishers and Booksellers Association in 1929.

As the latter example shows, even if the numbers of books indicted in the end turned out to be relatively small, the laws nevertheless had a devastating effect, leading to self-censorship and a public atmosphere of hate and harassment. Ultimately, it was the Nazis who profited.

6. When the Nazi book-burnings took place in May 1933, a substantial number of renowned writers and representatives of the cultural elite had already fled into exile. One writer who remained in Germany was Erich Kästner. Standing in the crowd, he was witness to the burning of his own books.

At a PEN Congress in 1958, Kästner, by then president of German PEN, commemorated the 25th anniversary of the book burnings and warned: "The events of 1933-1945 should have been fought in 1928. Later, it was too late. One must not wait until the fight for freedom is called treason. One must not wait until the snowball has turned into an avalanche. You have to crush the rolling snowball. Nobody will stop the avalanche... You can only fight rising dictatorships before they are in power."

Unfortunately, he did not leave a recipe as to how this could be achieved. It would be useful, even now. ⊗

*Hamburg-based **Regula Venske** is a crime writer and short-story writer. She is the winner of German crime-writing award (Deutscher Krimi Preis), and the current German PEN president*

"Media attacks are highest since 1989"

Politicians in South Africa threatened journalists in the run-up to the recent elections. **Natasha Joseph** reports on how editors are fighting back

48(02): 63/66 I DOI: 10.1177/0306422019858295

REPORTERS IN POST-APARTHEID South Africa are under "unprecedented" attack from politicians of all ideological stripes. Tensions soared in the run-up to the national and provincial elections on 8 May and the febrile atmosphere shows few signs of cooling down any time soon.

In the months leading up to the election, one of the most powerful figures in the governing African National Congress, deputy secretary-general Jessie Duarte, launched a blistering verbal attack on a journalist who'd asked a question about the party's controversial election candidates list. The reporter in question was described by Duarte on television as "a bully".

And it's not just the ANC, which just won the South African elections again, whose leaders have become increasingly hostile towards journalists. The opposition Economic Freedom Fighters have taken often vitriolic aim at the media. In one case, which prompted the South African National Editors Forum to launch a court challenge, EFF leader Julius Malema tweeted a message which contained political journalist Karima Brown's mobile phone number, claiming she was "sending moles" to a party event and supporting the ANC. Brown received death threats and rape threats on her phone after Malema's tweet went viral. He has since deleted the tweet.

These and other incidents prompted South African editors to take action. In late March,

with the elections just weeks away, SANEF unveiled an online tool designed to help journalists report instances of harassment, intimidation and violence – much of it expected to happen at the hands of political party leaders and supporters.

SANEF chairperson Mahlatse Mahlase, who is also an experienced political reporter and group editor-in-chief of Eyewitness News, told Index: "We wanted to start tracking cases and gathering numbers … what we have at the moment are mostly anecdotal reports [of journalists being targeted]."

William Bird is the director of Media Monitoring Africa, a watchdog and monitoring organisation that helped SANEF develop its harassment reporting tool. He told Index that the nature and degree of hostility directed at South African journalists in 2019 was "unprecedented in our democracy".

"I guess one element that has encouraged this – and [is] also linked to when it started – has been the rise of social media. As media models started to fall apart, as more stories were done by fewer journalists, as the relationships between journalists and their audiences started to decay as a result of these other elements, trust was eroded," he said. "At the same time, we suddenly saw an explosion of information: that anyone could now be a journalist was a potentially hugely democratising shift. But instead we have witnessed the potential of digital being subverted by those who seek to undermine media and democracy.

"At the same time, the pockets of excellence have exposed levels of corruption, malfeasance and greed last seen at these scales under apartheid and, as politicians the world over tend to, they shoot the messenger." All these factors

→

The message contained a single image: a gun etched with the phrase "stay classy"

CREDIT: Rogan Ward/Reuters

→ created what Bird calls "a perfect storm of declining trust, explosion of information, declining quality of reporting, breakdown of relationships and a society and nation going through hell, where just about everything needs some understanding and nuance".

Mahlase says that election periods were particularly fraught because of the now discredited machinations of the British PR firm Bell Pottinger, which were at their height after local government polls in 2016. Their clients, among others, were the Gupta family. The businessmen, who were close to then-President Jacob Zuma, have been implicated in a web of "state capture" that crippled large swathes of South Africa's government machinery and put the politics of patronage centre stage.

A key weapon in Bell Pottinger's armoury was Twitterbots. These "sock puppet accounts", as they were derisively called by many

The pockets of excellence have exposed levels of corruption, malfeasance and greed last seen at these scales under apartheid

but today it is used to target journalists who report critically."

And this, she warns, has "a chilling effect", especially on junior reporters. Given the abuse they see directed at others, "why would they pitch critical stories [of their own]?".

Her concern is echoed by journalist Qaanitah Hunter, who works for the Tiso Blackstar group, which counts South Africa's biggest-selling weekly newspaper, the Sunday Times, among its titles. She's had plenty of first-hand experience of intimidation and malice. In 2018, she received a WhatsApp message from a senior member of the ANC Women's League in response to questions she'd sent for an article. The message contained a single image: a gun etched with the phrase "stay classy".

Hunter told Index she had seen young, inexperienced journalists become increasingly cautious about tackling stories that involved powerful, politically connected people. "The consequence of this hostility to the media is self-censorship – and I think that is the biggest problem facing young journalists," she said.

"You don't want to wake up to the bots and trolls and the politicians singling you out, or being banned from events ... you don't want to deal with that. So what do you do? You stay away from the big stories, or you hunt with the mob. If everyone is hunting there, you stick with them instead of doing things that others aren't focusing on – the investigative work." It's not just individual journalists or media →

South Africans, targeted prominent journalists by accusing them of working for "white monopoly capital" – white businesspeople determined to undermine the black government – and being part of Stratcom, the former apartheid government's propaganda wing.

"Bell Pottinger created a well-orchestrated, well-funded campaign that used certain lingo to talk about journalists," said Mahlase. "We hadn't heard the term 'Stratcom' in decades,

In the same way the thugs gang together to attack, we need to stand together to defend

defend journalists." Bird concurs, and suggests that part of the solution lies in the very tools that have driven so much hostility toward the media. "Our digital reality offers huge potential to build rather than to undermine equality. But it will do so only if we make it do so," he said. "We need to make sure we take on the structural elements in an ongoing and comprehensive manner."

Bird, like Mahlase, says that solidarity beyond the media is key to turning the tide. "We should be asking our political leaders as a default where they stand on media freedom; we need to find a way of helping our media sector to stand together. If a party or group insults or attacks one journalist, it is an attack on all and we need to show solidarity with them. In the same way the thugs gang together to attack, we need to stand together to defend." ⊗

ABOVE: Current South African president Cyril Ramaphosa facing the press in 2013

→ houses that suffer in this scenario. Hunter added: "Hostility to the media leads to indifference among [audiences] – and has a chilling effect on whistleblowers."

So how can South Africa adapt to these grim realities? Mahlase said: "We shouldn't just accept this 25 years into our democracy. It's being presented as a battle of 'the media versus politicians', but South Africans need to understand that this is an attack on their right, as the public, to know – on our constitution. Anybody who loves democracy must step in to

Natasha Joseph *is a journalist and assistant editor at The Conversation Africa. She is based in Johannesburg, South Africa*

Big Brother's regional ripple effect

Kirsten Han reports on Singapore's new "fake news" law which allows ministers to restrict content and may embolden south-east Asian governments to clamp down on internet freedom

48(02): 67/69 I DOI: 10.1177/0306422019858296

LAWS PASSED IN May by the tiny city-state of Singapore to give ministers arbitrary powers to issue correction notices, order content removal, or block access to online content may spark a much wider clampdown in the region on internet freedom.

Journalists and human rights activists are worried that governments throughout south-east Asia will follow Singapore's lead and exploit concerns about fake news to introduce Draconian legislation – and that Singapore's use of such laws could legitimise similar action by even more authoritarian states, such as China.

"I expect we will next see copycat 'fake news' laws modelled on Singapore's law from the likes of Cambodia, Vietnam, Thailand, Myanmar, and other rights-repressing governments," said Phil Robertson, deputy director of Human Rights Watch's Asia division.

"Human rights-abusing ideas spread between governments [in south-east Asia] like the flu at a kindergarten."

The Protection from Online Falsehoods and Manipulation Act was introduced by Singapore's government in April, and pushed through via its parliamentary super-majority a month later. It allows any government minister, all of whom come from the People's Action Party which has been in power since 1959, the power to issue directives which can demand correction notices, content removal, and even the blocking of access to online content. The only criteria will be that the content contains statements that are "false or misleading" and the minister thinks it is in the "public interest" to do so.

Robertson told Index that the law also sought to apply restrictions to content communicated from outside the country if an end-user in Singapore could access it. This would allow ministers to force their judgments about what was "misleading" or "false" onto the wider internet, not just in south-east Asia but all around the world.

"Singapore is setting itself up to be Big Brother to censor and control internet posts and force 'corrections', and this will pose profound threats to freedom of expression and press freedom," he said.

This is an especially salient concern given Singapore's international reputation as one of the most outward-facing nations in the region.

The country is seen to have an efficient, highly-respected government, so the act's passage could legitimise the introduction of such laws among its neighbours. Political scientist Chong Ja-Ian is particularly worried about the effects on China. "The extra-territorial reach and restrictions of the law, if copied by significant entities like China, given the legitimisation that Singapore provides, could mean that these jurisdictions may be more able to pressure and restrict opinion abroad," he said.

As Tess Bacalla, executive director of the south-east Asian Press Alliance, said: "Other countries embarking on the same path as Singapore certainly do not need to copy the city-state's controversial draft law. But what it does is to embolden such states (as well as those contemplating the idea of enacting similar laws) to pursue the single-minded goal of silencing public voices, knowing full well they are not alone in this otherwise despicable endeavour."

Singapore's neighbours have already shown a willingness to clamp down on independent media outlets and harass journalists with arrests and lawsuits, as seen in countries such as Cambodia, where independent news outlets have been shut down, or in the Philippines, →

→ where journalists including Rappler's Maria Ressa find themselves kept busy with prosecutions and arrest warrants.

The state of press freedom is poor in the region. In the latest World Press Freedom Index, drawn up by Reporters Without Borders, six out of 11 south-east Asian countries had declined in the rankings.

Vietnam has introduced cyber-security laws that give the government power to compel social media companies to censor content, although it is not yet clear how the authorities are planning to enforce it. In the hands of such governments, a law like Pofma could allow critical reporting or criticism to be branded as "false statements" in need of "correction" or censorship on the grounds of broadly defined "public interest".

Pofma, as it has been enacted in Singapore, is pernicious because it can cause the shutdown of entire websites. If a website or page has received three such directives in a six-month period, any minister will be able to make it a "declared online location", the effect of which would be to ban the site from earning any revenue, be it through advertising, subscriptions, or even donations. On top of this, Pofma also allows ministers to exempt anyone they want from this law.

The act could also be bad news for Singapore's independent media scene, where alternative platforms that cover political news with a critical eye are already struggling to survive.

"Under the proposed law, three strikes and any one of the sites can be out. You need to go through legal appeal in order to overturn the ruling, and even if you are in the right, so what? What kind of publication can survive and start again afresh after being deprived of income and active readership, and the repeated threat of closure in the near future?" said Terry Xu, chief editor of The Online Citizen, a stalwart presence within the country's alternative media scene.

Unsurprisingly, this piece of legislation has attracted plenty of criticism from tech companies, international non-governmental organisations, academics, journalists, artists, writers, local civil society activists and even the United Nations special rapporteur for freedom of expression. Many of these critics have pointed to Singapore's already problematic record when it comes to press freedom and free speech, arguing that, in such a context, it would be unwise to grant the government more power to control the narrative. Singapore's law and home affairs minister, Kasiviswanathan Shanmugam, has sought to reassure Singaporeans, saying that

Human rights-abusing ideas spread between governments [in south-east Asia] like the flu at a kindergarten

CREDIT: Anne Derenne/Cartoon Movement

"99% of the people don't have to worry about what they do 99% of the time".

This hasn't done much to convince local activists. "The law was designed to crack down on critics the government doesn't like. This is their real intention," says civil rights activist Jolovan Wham. "Such assurances are false because laws affect everyone equally."

Even without a law like Pofma, Xu and his publication have already been accused of false or misleading reporting. Human Rights Watch's report on freedom of expression in Singapore, released in 2017, has also been denounced by the People's Action Party as a "deliberate falsehood".

But Xu isn't the only one who is alarmed. Criticism of the law came from a number of different fronts, most of which were taken aback by the bill's scope and the powers handed over to the government.

"By failing to distinguish between a malicious falsehood and a genuine mistake, the proposed legislation places an unnecessarily onerous burden on even journalists acting in good faith," a group of journalists wrote in an open letter addressed to the minister for communications and information, S Iswaran. Signatories to the letter include Clare Rewcastle Brown of the Sarawak Report; Andrew MacGregor Marshall, former Reuters deputy bureau chief in Bangkok; and former BBC, CNN and Al Jazeera English anchor Veronica Pedrosa.

"News organisations might feel compelled to withhold important stories simply because certain facts cannot be fully ascertained," the journalists added. "This is especially likely in Singapore, where it is often not possible to get a response in time from the government."

It isn't just press freedom that will be affected – human rights activists who monitor discrimination, marginalisation and abuses say their work could also be caught in the crosshairs. "My concerns are around LGBT survivors who suffered from institutional discrimination," said LGBT activist Jean Chong.

"With Pofma it could mean our words against theirs. And exposing state agencies could potentially become even more dangerous because any minister could, at his understanding of fake news and discretion, decide that we

The law was designed to crack down on critics the government doesn't like. This is their real intention

are lying and the state agencies are not."

While the Singapore government has pointed out that Pofma's provisions are in some aspects narrower than existing laws, which already allow for takedown orders or prosecutions, journalism professor Cherian George points out that more calibrated legislation isn't necessarily a cause for relief.

"China-style blocking is so extreme that the Singapore government has, sensibly, never used it against good-faith news media and blogs," he wrote in recent blog posts. "In contrast, Pofma would allow ministers to intervene in media cheaply. Considering the government's track record of overreaction, the temptation to play with this toy may prove irresistible."

In his defence of Pofma during its second reading, Shanmugam stood firm against the criticism and argued that the law would, in fact, be beneficial for democracy. He pointed to situations in countries such as the USA, claiming that misinformation had eroded public trust in their governments and institutions.

"Democracy is under serious threat. It is unwise for us to just watch and do nothing because it can sweep us over very quickly," he said.

Wham isn't buying this justification. "The law minister's claim that Pofma will preserve democracy is a joke and should be mocked for its stupidity," he said. "Which proper democracy in this world gives arbitrary powers to any minister to decide what's true or false and to compel takedowns and to force people to issue clarifications at their whim and fancy?" ⊗

Kirsten Han is a Singaporean freelance journalist and chief editor of New Naratif, a new platform for south-east Asian journalism, research, art and community-building

Who guards the writers?

Journalists in Italy are worried about losing their round-the-clock security. **Irene Caselli** finds out how this is affecting their lives and work

48(02): 70/73 I DOI: 10.1177/0306422019858297

IT HAS BEEN a year since Italy's new government took power. Deputy Prime Minister Matteo Salvini often appears in public wearing a police uniform and talks about security, but some writers feel their own security is under threat.

Salvini, who started his career as a reporter, is still a member of the Journalists' Guild. In May, Salvini said in a video: "A kiss to Saviano. I'm working on a revision of the criteria for the escorts that every day in Italy commit more than two thousand law enforcement workers." Roberto Saviano received death threats from the Neapolitan Mafia for his non-fiction book Gomorrah, and has 24-hour security.

Other writers and journalists, who live with 24-hour security, worry that they now risk losing their guards too.

"Those who have to be defended must be defended but police must not be drivers or personal assistants," Salvini said in April, adding that Italy's police escort system, *la scorta*, should be revised "to cut waste and unnecessary privileges".

Since Salvini, who leads the far-right League party and is also interior minister, came into power on 1 June 2018 in a coalition with the anti-establishment Five Star Movement (M5S), at least another two journalists have been put under 24-hour police escort, while veteran Mafia journalist Sandro Ruotolo had his 24-hour escort briefly removed and then reinstated.

For Paolo Berizzi, a reporter for the newspaper La Repubblica, Salvini's administration has had a direct impact on his security. Berizzi has been investigating Italy's far-right movements for 20 years, but he says that the worst threats have come recently, and have intensified with Salvini's escalation to power.

Since February, Berizzi's life has changed radically. What he misses most about his previous life without *la scorta* is being able to go for a run. He also finds it hard to do his job, having to co-ordinate all his movements in advance. During an interview with Index at the International Journalism Festival in Perugia, a plain-clothes policeman sits in one corner of the room, by the main door. He does not speak but his presence is far from invisible. The journalist's greatest worry is how this new level of security will affect his 13-year-old daughter.

"I can't pick up my daughter from school any more. If I want to go eat a pizza with my family, I need to work around it," Berizzi said, adding that for months his daughter had trouble sleeping. "When they put slogans in my building, my daughter was traumatised, because they violated our private space. She has access to the internet; she can read about the threats.

"It is a paradox that the ministry of the interior decided to put a reporter under police escort, when the same ministry is led by a political leader that has been in cahoots with

BELOW: Journalist Paolo Berizzi who investigates the far-right has received an increasing number of threats since the current government took power

IL MINISTRO

these far-right groups. Salvini has gone hunting for their votes, has used their slogans and their clothes, and has made them feel part of the public life of this country. This was not the case up until a few years ago," Berizzi said.

Floriana Bulfon, a freelance journalist who has written about Rome's Casamonica crime clan, among other things, told Index: "I feel more vulnerable to the extent that we have a minister [Salvini] who worries about fighting with Saviano and another one [Luigi Di Maio] that threatens to close down newspapers." Bulfon is under the first level of police protection, where she gets mobile police patrols checking on her house and police officers with her at meetings. In March, after previous threats and attacks, she found a bottle containing an inflammable liquid inside her car. She sees no direct connection between this episode and the current administration but says that, overall,

The door to his house was set on fire, and last year news emerged of a Mafia plan to murder him

things have worsened for journalists such as her. "I worry about the future of press freedom. It is something that you build over time, and you can [damage] it."

Paolo Borrometi, a Sicilian journalist who has been attacked by the Mafia and who now lives under round-the-clock protection, told Index: "Something dramatic is happening in Italy: we are not outraged anymore when a journalist is threatened. It is unacceptable." The changing political climate appears to have had a wide range of ramifications for

ABOVE: Deputy Prime Minister Matteo Salvini dressed in police uniform, talking in Afragola, Italy, after a series of attacks in the north of Naples

There are no norms in Italy to guarantee freedom of the press

→ journalists. Despite reporting on neo-fascist groups for a long time, it was not until 2017 that Berizzi received some police protection. This happened after he found a swastika and a crucifix scratched on his car, which was parked outside his house in the northern city of Bergamo. The threats continued. In Padua, a presentation of his book NazItalia was interrupted by fascist squads. In October 2018, he found a message painted in his block of flats saying: "Berizzi, traitor, you will pay". Last February, his police surveillance was turned into a 24-hour police detail.

It is the Central Interagency Office for Personal Security (UCIS), an independent body of the ministry of the interior, that assigns *la scorta* following an analysis of threat levels. UCIS was set up in 2002 after a labour law professor, Marco Biagi, was killed by a group linked to Red Brigade terrorists shortly after his police escort was pulled. UCIS can assign low-level protection or a round-the-clock escort.

In December, Salvini was photographed shaking the hand of Luca Lucci, a notorious far-right AC Milan supporting football hooligan accused of bodily harm and sentenced to one-and-a-half years for drug-dealing. Salvini said he has his picture taken with hundreds of fans and had never seen Lucci before. He did, however, adopt the "Italians First" slogan from far-right activist group CasaPound, and has used several slogans from the fascist era.

On the July 2018 anniversary of Benito Mussolini's birth, Salvini tweeted a newspaper piece about those who criticised him, and said: "So many enemies, so much honour." The words echoed Mussolini's infamous phrase of "Many Enemies, Much Honour". In May, he came under fire for addressing his supporters in the central town of Forlì from the same balcony where Mussolini witnessed his opponents' executions.

Salvini has shrugged off accusations of wanting to emulate Mussolini, and has called fascists "idiots" on several occasions. Apologies for fascism are illegal in Italy if proven to be part of an attempt to recreate the defunct Fascist Party.

But Berizzi sees a clear connection between the current political landscape and the threats against him. "If in 2019, 100 years after the creation of the Italian Fasci of Combat, a journalist is forced to live and work under police escort because of political reasons, and not because of Mafia threats, this is a sign of what is happening in the country," Berizzi said, referring to Mussolini's 1919 set-up of the precursor of the National Fascist Party that brought him to power in 1921.

It is unclear how many journalists live under police protection in Italy at the moment. The latest official figures go back to February 2018, when the government said 176 journalists received protection while 19 were under 24-hour police escort. Since then, Berizzi and Marilù Mastrogiovanni, who is under threat from the Mafia in the southern region of Puglia, have been added to the list.

A worrying development took place in May 2019 when Stefano Origone, a journalist for La Repubblica, was badly beaten by police during clashes between the neo-fascist CasaPound movement and anti-fascist protesters in Genoa. He had clearly identified himself as a reporter.

A recent report considered Italy's situation to be "particularly worrying". The Council of Europe's Platform for the Protection of Journalism and Safety of Journalists, whose partner organisations include Index on Censorship, said Italy was the EU member state with the highest number of active threats in 2018, with violations having tripled compared to the previous year. The report added: "The majority of alerts recorded in 2018 have been submitted after the official installation of the new coalition government on 1 June. The government's two deputy prime ministers, Luigi Di Maio and Matteo Salvini, regularly express through social media rhetoric particularly hostile to the media and journalists." Di Maio, leader of the M5S, has called journalists "worthless jackals" and has said it is high time newspapers closed down.

"Living with *la scorta* is no privilege," said Borrometi, who is also the president of Articolo 21, an association that promotes the constitutional principle of freedom of expression. "Thinking it is a privilege is distorting reality."

Borrometi has been beaten by two hooded men, who left his back injured. The door to his house was set on fire, and last year news emerged of a Mafia plan to murder him.

He says that while personal attacks have worsened under the current administration, things have been difficult for journalists for a long time. "There are no norms in Italy to guarantee freedom of the press," he said. He points out that previous governments didn't scrap a defamation law which serves as a de facto gag: the Italian penal code guarantees prison sentences of up to six years for the criminal defamation of a politician – a policy that has been heavily criticised by international rights groups. "The breakdown of trust comes from afar, and it culminates in this administration that has an unacceptable spirit of violence against journalists," he said. "It is outrageous. These are not threats against single individuals. Our job is fundamental to inform citizens. Every citizen's freedom is at stake." ⊗

Irene Caselli is a contributing editor for Index on Censorship magazine. She is based in Monte Castello di Vibio, Italy

"Della mafia conosco solo quello che conoscono tutti. Giornali e televisioni non fanno che parlar di mafia. La cupola? Io conosco solo le cupole delle chiese... Il personaggio sanguinario che mi hanno disegnato su misura è falso. [...] La droga mi fa schifo solo a parlarne."

Michele Greco, boss di Cosa Nostra

ABOVE: Writer Roberto Saviano who lives under 24-hour police protection. He is showing a quote from the notorious Cosa Nostra boss Michele Greco denying any knowledge of the Mafia

LEFT: Italian Deputy Prime Minister Matteo Salvini poses with a machine gun in Rome in October 2018

China in their hands

Chinese author and journalist **Xinran** reflects on the impact of China's social credit system

48(02): 74/76 | DOI: 10.1177/0306422019858298

I SAW A PHOTOGRAPH published in a Chinese newspaper earlier this year. It was of a queue of people, who looked as though they were in a line for welfare payouts or buying the latest mobile phone.

But this was something different. This was a crowd of people turning themselves in at a police station in Hainan Province. The story claimed that 299 people surrendered themselves at the same police station in one day, and that this scene appeared repeatedly across the province.

Between February and April 2019, the police cracked down on telecommunication network fraud, and during that period many "criminals" turned themselves in.

This surprising development was partly because of the pressure of the introduction of a new social credit system, which is being used by the Chinese government to judge people's actions and award them scores for doing things the state sees as positive or negative. Social credit scoring is a new way of driving people to take particular actions in order to improve their rating with the government. If they do things that the government believes is not in the public interest individuals risk bad scores.

The social credit system started in 2014, and by 2020 it is estimated that the social behaviour of 1.4 billion Chinese will be tracked by modern data technology, using facial recognition and other systems to follow each person's social behaviour as a basis for reward and punishment.

Chinese leaders believe that the social credit system is an attempt to prove to the masses that government decision-making is based on data analysis, thereby enhancing public trust of the government to regulate corporate and private behaviour. It gives the state the ability to use big data to define people's daily behaviour; to supervise people's social behaviour in a more detailed, comprehensive and accurate manner; and to set a score on their record. The scores can affect even people's daily food and lodgings.

The social credit system originated as an economic model in the West in the early 20th century and is the basis of credit scoring in many countries. Agencies gather information about individuals and businesses to establish their creditworthiness and that can affect whether they can get services such as loans and mortgages. Even shopping websites and taxi firms issue ratings, upon which future transactions can depend. But this is different from the way it is being applied in China.

An episode of the British TV series Black Mirror explains how such a system could control social behaviour. In one episode, Nosedive, the heroine is very friendly to everyone, so she gets a rating of 4.2. In order to get a higher score, she painstakingly pleases others, and finally gets to go to a wedding which will help her. But on her way there, the flight gets cancelled. The woman becomes angry and argues with airport staff, so the security guards punish her. Her score plummets to one star, and she is eventually arrested by the police.

When Confucius designed China's national governance system for the country's rulers 2,500 years ago, he emphasised that "faith, loyalty, honesty, food, and military" were the five key factors.

However, since 1911, when China ended imperial rule, the traditional concepts and system of honesty has withered and been eroded by endless wars and political storms. The Chinese who lost their beliefs and direction are like worker ants who have lost their queen. When Mao Zedong took over the country in 1949, he set up "the personal political file" for everyone, but no one other than governors were allowed to see them.

Whether they were for work assignments, school selection or political review, these lifelong personnel files became the basis for rewards and punishments.

Using the private and opaque nature of the files, government officials often engaged in favouritism and other forms of unlawful conduct, even adding fake information in acts of personal vengeance.

My mother, who is 86, has told me that in her lifetime, countless people have been killed because of their political files, and many people have been punished without knowing why. Living in fear and dying for unknown reasons was a way of life for three generations in China.

During China's "Reform and Opening Up" period in the 1980s Deng Xiaoping started to relax rules from the previous period to encourage economic growth. But independent judicial and legal education had not yet recovered from the 30 years of political strangulation, and lawless speculators became the first group to benefit from economic "openness". The majority of the Chinese *Lao-Bai-Xin* (common people) began to grasp chances to find new ways to make money, hoping for a better life. During this period, I believe, trust

and traditional Chinese values were polluted by the desire for money.

British-Chinese businessman Tim Clissold, the author of Mr China, who has been working with Chinese companies since 1990s, said that if President Xi Jinping wants to maintain the absolute leadership of the Communist Party and protect its right to formulate and implement its strategy, he cannot allow the introduction of the Western judicial system so that ordinary people can sue the government.

The social credit system is an enforcement mechanism whereby individual rights are controlled by state rights, says Clissold. This is controversial in the West, but many →

ABOVE: A boy plays with a ribbon while under the watchful eye of a security camera near Tiananmen Square, China. An estimate in 2018 suggested that the Chinese government had already installed close to 200 million surveillance cameras across the country

It is estimated that the social behaviour of 1.4 billion Chinese will be tracked by modern data technology, using facial recognition and other systems to follow each person's social behaviour as a basis for reward and punishment

WHAT IS CHINA WATCHING?

|||||||||||||||||||||||||||||||||||||||||||||||||||||

- China's police is expected to spend $30 billion on surveillance in the upcoming years, according to state media
- In 2017, the BBC sent journalist John Sudworth to Guiyang, a southern city with a population of 3.5 million people to see if he could get lost in the crowd – it took just seven minutes for cameras to detect Sudworth as a "suspect"
- There are up to 30 million individuals, including suspected terrorists, criminals, drug traffickers, political activists and others, who are flagged for watching in the national database
- Police have arrested 4,000 people since the start of 2016 through the use of facial recognition surveillance, including 1,000 in Hangzhou
- It is estimated there will be 450 million surveillance cameras in China by 2020, which is more than double the amount of cameras operating in 2018

Sources: New York Times, BBC, The Atlantic, Washington Post

→ Chinese do not care about its human-rights significance.

Some believe that this system can at least improve transparency, resolve transaction disputes between enterprises, and regulate people's social behaviour, so that overall efficiency and equity can improve. However, the improvement and independence of China's judiciary is one of the fundamental problems that this fast-developing country urgently needs to solve, he says.

American-Chinese author Fan Wu has just returned to the UK from China. She is working on a new book about the country's younger generation. She told me that in recent years, the Chinese government has tightened ideological and thought control even more to strengthen Xi's administration, partly using propaganda banners and also via China's online networks Sina, Douban and Youku.

But, on the other hand, social media such as WeChat, Douyin and Weibo are also immensely popular. People still often use them to vent their dissatisfaction and frustration towards the government, and it won't be surprising if China's central government wants to monitor social media even more closely in future.

I would like to know if China's social credit system is to give the trustworthy "sweet benefits" and give those who show bad behaviour "painful punishment"? What is the principle that the social credit system is based on? Is it based on internationally-recognised law or on the Communist Party's rules? If a citizen criticises the government, is her or his social credit reduced? How does this system protect people's privacy and personal faith? Would Chinese journalists' daily work also be included in the credit system one day?

I really hope the young Chinese people of the future don't have to live in fear and panic as my mother and I have both had to. But I worry that this social credit system has the potential to make them do just that. ⊗

Xinran is an author and journalist. Her latest book is The Promise: Love and Loss in Modern China (I.B. Tauris)

Playing out injustice

Musician and opposition politician **Bobi Wine** talks to **Lewis Jennings** about striking a chord with Ugandan youth

48(02): 77/77 | DOI: 10.1177/0306422019858299

We talk about the injustice that happens. When you put it into music it awakens the people

"**THEY CLAIM WE** are too young to get involved with the politics of our country but we are not too young to face the injustices, so music is really important to wake up the people and stand up to the occasion," said Ugandan singer Bobi Wine.

Wine's lyrics are sung to an upbeat melody of ragga dancehall, a popular style of music that originates from Jamaica. They had a haunting resonance when, in May, he was arrested and charged for protesting last year against Uganda's social media tax which charges Ugandans for going onto social networking sites.

He was released on bail, while a hashtag campaign, #FreeBobiWine, went viral during his imprisonment.

"It's very important to get our message across to young people in Uganda because the regime was able to successfully keep young people away from the politics," 37-year-old Wine told Index.

Wine, whose real name is Robert Kyagulanyi, has a huge following as a musician and as leader of the People Power party. He speaks for many young people in Uganda and his outspoken lyrics and activism have led to him being repeatedly arrested.

"We talk about the injustice that happens," said Wine. "When you put it into music it awakens the people and they get concerned about the government of their country. We have a following and music is [how] we get in touch with the people. We create awakening and tell them to take responsibility for their country."

Wine, who joined parliament as an independent in 2017, is a prominent critic of President Yoweri Museveni. More than 120 of his concerts in 2017 were cancelled by security forces, who use teargas and water cannons to break up his rallies. A draft censorship law, often referred to as the "anti-Bobi Wine law", demonstrates the threat the authorities consider him to be. The law places various restrictions on artists and filmmakers, including making them seek government approval for song lyrics and for when they want to perform abroad.

"If I have to travel outside [the country] to perform, I have to ask for permission," he said. "If I have to shoot a video, I have to ask for permission. They did all that to stop [me] and limit [me] from reaching the people musically [but] by doing that, it affected the whole music industry." ⊗

Lewis Jennings *is editorial assistant at Index on Censorship*

BELOW: Ugandan musician Bobi Wine visits the Kibera slums in Kenya, October 2018. Wine is known for leading a political party called People Power

PICTURED: A pro-choice supporter reacts to senators voting against the legalisation of abortion outside the National Congress in Buenos Aires, Argentina during August 2018

CULTURE

"Watch out, we're going to disappear you"

Argentinian author **Claudia Piñeiro** tells **Irene Caselli** how her call for legal abortions led to campaigns of intimidation and calls for her novels to be boycotted

48(02): 80/83 I DOI: 10.1177/0306422019857913

LEFT: A portrait of Argentinian writer Claudia Piñeiro

WHEN ARGENTINIAN NOVEL-IST and playwright Claudia Piñeiro started speaking out in favour of a law to legalise abortion, the backlash was violent.

The first attacks came online. She received messages that included the image of a green Ford Falcon, the car used by death squads during the 1976-83 military regime.

"I thought that we had settled certain issues in Argentina, especially regarding the military dictatorship," Piñeiro told Index. "I thought we all agreed: we put those responsible on trial, we said never again. But then someone, with impunity, sends you a picture of a green Falcon and says: 'Watch out, we're going to disappear you.' I was really surprised. I didn't think there were still people who thought

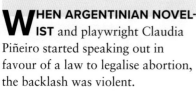

The word 'abortion' was forbidden for a long time

that the dictatorship was a possible method, that it could come back."

In July 2018, just before Argentina's senate was set to hold a historic vote on the legalisation of abortion, an online campaign called for a boycott of Piñeiro's novels and tried to get her excluded from a literary panel. Piñeiro was due to moderate a conversation with Cuban author Leonardo Padura at an event organised by Argentina's private health insurance provider Osde.

"There were days that more than 200 people called Osde to get me kicked out of that job [moderating the event]," said Piñeiro. "The argument was that I was an abortionist. But it was a job that had nothing to do with abortion."

Women's rights organisations and her publishing house, Penguin Random House, came out in support and said they would fight attempts at censorship. Thanks to the support, she eventually presented the talk.

"It was quite worrying. I didn't think that in my country there were people who were willing to censor you and take a job away from you

because you think differently from them," she said.

The theme of abortion has also appeared in Piñeiro's work, including in Basura para las Gallinas (Rubbish for the Hens), translated here for the first time into English for Index. The short story tells of a mother who helps her daughter to abort her baby at home.

It is inspired by reality: in Latin America, 97% of women of reproductive age live under restrictive abortion laws.

The word "abortion" never appears in Basura para las Gallinas. "The word 'abortion' was forbidden for a long time," Piñeiro said. "We would use euphemisms to refer to it. It was taboo."

She wrote the story eight years ago, before the movement to legalise abortion gained momentum. Although the senate eventually rejected the bill in August 2018, the topic remains a hot potato and a new bill was introduced on 28 May.

"It is awful that while we have MPs who are so backward and so dependent on the favours they exchange with the churches, we are going to have women who die of abortion in Argentina," said Piñeiro. "But in a while it will not happen anymore. Today, abortion is spoken of more naturally. Even if it is still illegal, it is no longer prohibited in the language." ⊗

Irene Caselli *is a contributing editor to Index on Censorship*

Rubbish for the Hens

SHE PREPARES TO tie the black plastic bag. She tugs the strings to make the knot. But they're too short, she put too much into that bag, she doesn't even know what, nor how much she's stuffed inside to fill it – everything she found as she walked round and round the house.

She lifts the bag by its edges and shakes it up and down so that the weight of the rubbish compresses the contents and frees up more space for the knot. She ties it twice, two knots. She checks that the bow is firm by tugging the plastic loops to each side. The knot tightens and doesn't come undone.

She sets the bag aside and washes her hands. She turns on the tap and lets the water run while she pours detergent onto her hands. When she was a girl, they didn't have detergent at home, they used white soap if there was any. Now she has detergent – she brings it home from what they buy by the barrel at work. She fills an empty soda bottle and sticks it in her backpack. They didn't have plastic bags either when she was a girl, her grandmother put all the leftovers or scraps that could serve to fertilise the earth or feed the chickens into a bucket and they burned everything else behind the fence, on the earthen track. Into the bucket went the potato peelings, the apple cores, the rotted lettuce, the overripe tomatoes, the eggshells, the brewed maté leaves, the chicken entrails, their hearts, the fat. Since she lives in the city, however, she uses plastic bags, reused shopping bags or bags bought specifically to contain rubbish like the one she's just tied. She sticks all the leftovers and rubbish into a single bag without separating them, because where she lives now there are no chickens, nor land to be fertilised.

She shuts off the tap and dries her hand with a dry cloth. She looks at the alarm clock that she left that afternoon on top of the fridge, it's time to put the bag out on the street for the rubbish lorry to take away. She walks down the narrow hallway all the neighbours share. Dangling from her left hand she carries the bag, held tight by the knot. She must leave the bag on the pavement just a few minutes before the binmen pass by. In her right hand she carries the handful of keys that weighs almost as much as the bag. The metal keyring is a cube with the logo of the cleaning company she works for, and from its silvered circle hang the keys to this building and those of each of the five offices she cleans; the keys of a previous job where she no longer works; the two keys of the door towards which she's walking now, with the rubbish bag banging against her leg as she moves; the key to the door of her house, ground floor in the back; that of the basement where they store the bicycle her husband uses to go to work when he has a job; and that of the door to her daughter's room, which she's just added to the keyring after locking it.

When she reaches the door to the street she turns the handle but it doesn't open, she leaves the bag on the ground and works her way around the ring, key by key, until she reaches the right one. She sticks the key in the lock and opens the door. First one door and then the other. The second key was added after thieves got into apartment H. She keeps the door open with a foot while →

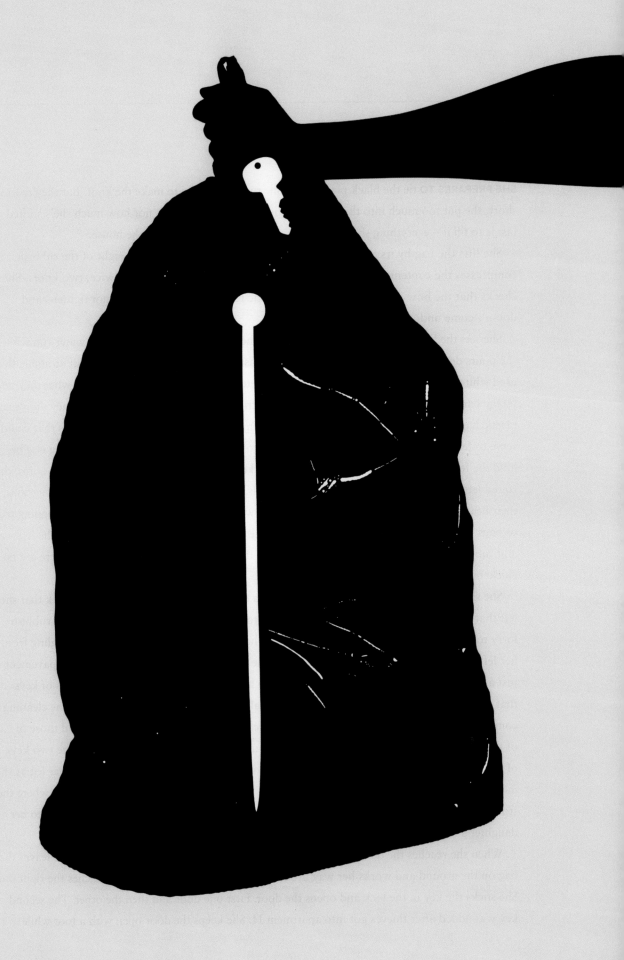

→ she picks the bag up once more. On this short trajectory to the tree where she will leave it for the binmen, she carries it hugged against her chest. In embracing it she realises that the knitting needle broke the plastic and is aimed at her, as if pointing at her. She looks at it but doesn't touch it. She turns the bag so that the metal needle no longer points at her.

When she reaches the tree she sets the bag on the ground again, beside other bags that others left before her. With her foot she pushes the needle so it goes inside the bag from which it shouldn't have poked out. The needle goes in until it hits something and then she can't push it any further lest it poke out the other side and wind up make things worse. She remains watching the hole the needle had made, expecting to see a viscous liquid coming through it, but the liquid doesn't flow out. If it were to do so, and someone were to ask her, she'd say it was from any of the other things she threw inside to fill the bag. But nothing comes out of the hole.

She plays with the keys as she waits for the rubbish lorry. She spins the keys one by one around the ring. It is night-time although the afternoon is still not over, the cold of July biting her face. She rubs her arms to warm herself. She shakes the keyring as if it were a rattle. That's it, its ending. She wishes she could go back inside her house to see how her daughter is, but she can't leave the bag there alone. She fears someone sniffing in her rubbish in search of something that might be of use. Or a dog, attracted by the scent. She knows that animals can smell things that we humans can't. Where she lived with her grandmother there were animals, dogs, a donkey, chickens, once they even had a pig.

She is cold but can't go and let some dog voraciously attack the bag she's just taken out for the binmen. In her grandmother's house there were three dogs. Her grandmother also used a needle, but not the plastic bag, instead one of the two buckets. What her sister expelled went into the bucket for the chickens. She saw her grandmother remove it from her sister, that's how she knows how to do it: to stick in the needle, wait, the cries, the bellyaches, the blood, and then gathering what came out into the bucket and throwing it to the hens. She learned by watching her grandmother. And that's how she did it today, just as she remembered.

Only this time it will turn out better, because she now knows what she needs to do if her daughter shouts out in pain and doesn't stop bleeding. She knows where to bring her. Her daughter won't die. In the city it's different, there are hospitals or medical clinics nearby. Her grandmother didn't know what to do, there was no place to take her sister.

Where they lived there hadn't been anything, not even neighbours. There were no bunches of keys that opened and closed so many doors. There were no people sorting through what others left behind. No plastic bags. There was nothing. But there were chickens, who ate up the trash.

....

Translated by **Lawrence Schimel**

Claudia Piñeiro *is an Argentinian novelist and screenwriter, best known for her crime writing. She is the winner of the Sor Juana Inés de la Cruz Prize*

"Knowing that they are there, helps me keep smiling in my cell"

LEFT: Turkish journalist and author Ahmet Altan at the Edinburgh Book Festival, Scotland, in August 2015

Index interviews best-selling novelist and former newspaper editor **Ahmet Altan** from his prison cell in Turkey about his writing and his family tradition of dissent

48(02): 84/88 | DOI: 10.1177/0306422019857914

EVEN IN THE days when novelist and journalist Ahmet Altan was free, he was always politically lonely in Turkey. His long-time anti-militarism, his liberal instincts and embrace of ethnic and religious minorities in the country have made him powerful enemies in both the old secular establishment and the new religious one.

But his jailing in 2016 and subsequent life sentence on spurious charges relating to a failed military coup have left him even more friendless. As commentator Rusen Cakir put it recently: "Few, other than his close friends and relatives, remember him [in jail] because the number of people who dislike Altan on both sides of the political polarisation in Turkey is tremendously high."

"At the moment, thousands of people are jailed on illegal and illogical charges. Kurdish politicians, leftists and opposition religious people have all had their share of this lawlessness," Altan told Index from prison.

"I came out against the unlawful practices of both the era of military tutelage and that of the AKP [the ruling Justice and Development Party]: I believe I am a target of their anger."

Dissent is something of an Altan family tradition. Ahmet's father, Çetin, was a parliamentarian on the far left who served two years in prison for his journalism, and had

his writing featured in early issues of Index, while his brother, Mehmet, is now serving a life sentence alongside him on similar charges.

Ahmet Altan was given a suspended sentence of one year and eight months in 1995 for a column that parodied Turkish civic nationalism by imagining an alternate reality in which Mustafa Kemal Ataturk, the founder of the modern nation, had been born Kurdish and founded a country called Kurdey. Over the rest of his journalistic career he faced continual charges on grounds ranging from raising the Armenian genocide to insulting the president.

"In the era of military tutelage, my father coined the name 'shell state'. There was the image of a state but it was empty," Altan said.

"We wanted to fill the inside of that shell with democracy and law. The AKP came to power promising they would do this. But when they established themselves in government, they broke the shell to pieces. There is no longer even the image of a state and law."

Taraf, a newspaper at which Altan was editor-in-chief from 2007-12, became known for its reporting of scandals involving military attempts to claw back power from the Islamist government. However, Altan said that some soldiers tried on coup

Tell readers that their existence gives thousands of people in prison like me the strength to go on

charges back then were also mistreated by the legal system.

"They were tried in a legal order established on the belief that it would only try opposition figures," he said. "Conditions change and the system you have established to try the opposition also does you an injustice. That is no good to anyone."

Yasemin Çongar, a former colleague at Taraf who recently translated a book by Altan about his experiences in prison, told Index that

he was "as full of life as ever, not only coping with utterly unjust treatment but also turning his time in prison into a life-affirming experience".

Altan said he was using the time to put the finishing touches to another novel. "Tell readers that their existence gives thousands of people in prison like me the strength to go on," he said. "Knowing that they are there, helps me keep smiling in my cell."

Below, we print an extract from

The Longest Night translated into English by Index for the first time. Altan's novel tells the love story of an Istanbul couple torn apart when one joins an EU anthropological research group in the remote mountains of south-east Turkey, a Kurdish-majority area under military control.

The novel sold a million copies when it was published in 2005. In this chapter, two history researchers argue about whether to write a book about the Armenian genocide. ⊗

The Longest Night

SELIM WAS AT ease in those days; his soul was as tranquil as the warm spring noontimes. Like a man who had escaped a serious illness, he picked out the details of the diary of his life with joy, and only sought out small pleasures. When he left the school where he worked, he would go straight back home, put flowers bought from gypsies into a vase, and sit alone on his balcony. He would make himself salads out of unusual plants, cook up dishes he had tasted in strange places in his childhood, read a travel magazine, look over the documents Mahmut had found, and watch a film. He wasn't in contact with any women: not even Fahrünisa.

Sometimes he would drink beer and argue about history with Mahmut, talking about how heavy the burden of knowing the truth was in a place where recent history was almost entirely a lie from top to bottom and asking how they could manage to stay honest in a profession that did not allow them to reveal what was true... They had a dream of writing a history book together that would lay out all the truths of what had happened in the first quarter of the 20th century.

"Where would we get this book published?" Mahmut asked.

"That's not the real problem," Selim replied. "The real problem is where we will live after the book is published. People are so drenched in lies that no one will believe the truths we tell. They'll think we're lying. We'll be everyone's enemy – they won't let us live here."

They would imagine what the table of contents would look like, which gave them a professional pleasure even greater than talking history.

"We'll write this book in the end," Selim said one day. "I can't go any longer without telling people what I know about this. And I know you can't either."

"Will we leave here after that?"

"I don't know... Let's write the book first, then worry about that. Let's begin slowly sorting through the documents."

→ Mahmut laughed.

"You mean I'll start sorting through the documents... I'll get tired of you one day, I'll have you know!"

"Your Highness Sultan Mahmut the Third, you are saddening the people with your threatening pronouncements..."

The idea of writing a book lit up Selim's tranquil inner world, entertained his intellect and pushed his sadness over Yelda a little further back in his mind, although sometimes he was unexpectedly overcome by the tremors it caused.

Once, while driving to school... It could have been a love song on the radio or maybe the long-repressed passion that had unconsciously become a part of him breaking out of the cocoon in which it had been trapped, but he had been struck by a sudden crisis of longing. This was no normal feeling of yearning – at that moment he so violently wanted to see Yelda's face and hear her voice that his chest tightened and the steering wheel seemed to jump out of its position and push against his ribcage. He pulled the car to one side and stopped. He felt that his whole body

---

Sometimes he would drink beer and argue about history with Mahmut, talking about how heavy the burden of knowing the truth was in a place where recent history was almost entirely a lie from top to bottom

---

had gone a pallid grey from this hopeless longing. For a second, he considered getting straight back onto the road and going to Yelda, but he became even more depressed by the thought that, even if he started out now, he would not be able to reach her in less than a day. His head resting on the steering wheel, he repeated to himself: "This will pass, this will pass".

One or two hours later the longing had subsided, but then another sigh opened up a new pain.

When, in that short time, he became so strongly aware of the heartache that his longing and loneliness had fostered – and how it had enveloped his body, leaving him feeling like a prisoner in a cage of infeasibilities, how he had become bogged down in the wretchedness of never being able to see the person he wanted to see, and how hopeless he felt, the inadequacy of knowing that deciding to go and see someone would not be enough to be able to see her – he had remembered Yelda's heartbroken voice saying: "I have missed you". With the memory of that sound, he let out an involuntary wail as though somewhere was hurting.

"Does Yelda feel this every day?" he asked himself. "How does she live with the pain?"

He could not even stand the thought of Yelda suffering. He wanted to phone her right there →

→ and then and tell her: "Get ready. I am coming to get you. We will be together for the rest of our lives – I will make that fairy tale come true." If he had known that he were able to reach her, maybe he would not have been able to stop himself and he would have called.

He knew they were in the worst situation in which two people who loved each other could be: their love was alive enough that it would never be lost, but the relationship between them had rotted and fallen through like an old bridge, leaving them on different banks of the same river. They could see but not reach one another, and when they shouted out to one another most of their words were drowned out by the wind.

Despite all that he felt, he believed that that bridge could never be rebuilt – indeed, he no longer had the strength to try: their relationship, and their souls, had been left terminally ill by those fights, jealousies, and unfading doubts.

He would not tell Yelda about that dreadful fit of passion in the car, how he had pulled over to the side of the road and how his breath was cut short by the violence of his longing, and Yelda would not know how much he missed her.

He had thought that Yelda going far away had hastened and eased the breaking up of their relationship, that this had been better for both of them, and had avoided the conversations that could have made this break-up harder by uncovering and nourishing the love between them.

Two souls that had loved one another, that had hurt one another, and whose passion for one another had been uncovered may have thought that they would be able simply to break that bond, but those who succumb to this lovesickness do not know how difficult it is to part.

On that dreadful morning, when he had left the house after reading Yelda's emails, he had fallen into the same error. For days he had called her, frightened that something might have happened to her, sometimes 20 times in a row, but the phone was never answered. He had been afraid that she might have died or something terrible might have happened to her, but after finding out from a common friend that she was well he had decided that it was over, and even felt a little satisfaction as he ceased calling.

At that time, he had also gone through a period of calm – like the present.

One day, one month later, Yelda called him.

"I need to talk to you."

Selim had paused with misgivings that the relationship would reignite, and then Yelda had spoken in that heartbroken voice.

"Come over... I would see it as a favour to me. You should as well."

He was unable to resist her tone of surrender.

"I'm on my way now," he said.

....

Ahmet Altan is an acclaimed journalist and one of Turkey's most read novelists. Currently he is imprisoned for life in his home country

A rebel writer

Sally Gimson talks to Egyptian writer
Eman Abdelrahim about mental illness,
surrealism and smoking in public

48(02): 89/94 | DOI: 10.1177/0306422019857915

LEFT: Short-story writer
Eman Abdelrahim

EMAN ABDELRAHIM BELONGS to a new generation of Egyptian short-story writers shaped by the country's uprising and the internet.

Although she declines to call herself either a feminist or a political activist, her stories tell of the struggles of Arab women to find their place in a world where they are torn between the conservative society they were brought up in and the liberation which events such as the Arab Spring promised. Her tales also touch on taboo subjects like mental illness.

Her short story Laugh and the World Laughs with Me, an extract of which is published in English below, is the intimate story of a woman who has a schizophrenic brother. It is set against the backdrop of the demonstrations in Tahrir Square.

The main character, Fadwa, works as a presenter for the BBC Arabic Service and the 2011 uprising, playing out on the television in the family's flat, provides a soundtrack to the domestic action. But her brother, Shadi, is plagued by demons. He believes there are secret messages being sent to him through the news.

Fadwa is struggling between her job, her domestic obligations to her brother and father and her desire to take part in the revolution happening in the streets.

Many of Abdelrahim's stories present women's dilemmas in surreal ways. She tells tales of brides in black, secret staircases and threatening male strangers in wolf masks. Her first short-story collection, Rooms and Other Stories, won her accolades including a Sawaris Cultural Award for emerging writers in 2015. The literary website Lithub identified her as one of the top 10 female Arab writers who should be translated into English.

Her main influences are the Russian greats Anton Chekhov, Nikolai Gogol and Fyodor Dostoevsky, and she sees parallels between Egyptian society today and 19th century Tsarist Russia.

Now 37, Abdelrahim started writing anonymous blogs in her early 20s. The daughter of a teacher and a nurse, she lived with her parents and five younger siblings in Riyadh, Saudi Arabia, until she was 15.

The family was plunged into crisis when her father was killed in a car accident shortly after they all returned to Cairo. Her mother had no way of supporting them and remarried quickly. She divorced after setting up her own property business.

Abdelrahim completed university, where she studied business, and worked for an import-export company. She wrote in her spare time, moving from writing blogs to finding her voice composing fictional stories on Facebook. Encouraged by her friends, she used her dreams as inspiration. She was rebelling, too. She took off her hijab, curled her hair – and then cut it all off.

"I was at war with everything. I was conservative and I became the opposite," she explained. "I used to smoke in public. This was a big problem... a big thing."

People in the street used to think that, because of the way she looked and behaved, she must be a foreigner. She also became mentally ill and her psychiatrist encouraged her to write as a way of healing.

Now married to a German anthropologist, she lives in Chemnitz and is writing stories inspired by her mother, who died last year.

But Abdelrahim is still surprised that she's a writer. "I loved writing. Nothing else," she said. "I never considered anyone would read it. I am writing for me as a reader."

The extract from Abdelrahim's short story Laugh and the World Laughs with Me is published below. ⊗

Sally Gimson is deputy editor of Index on Censorship Magazine

I used to smoke in public. This was a big problem... a big thing

Laugh and the World Laughs with Me

ON THE WEDNESDAY night, the President delivers his second speech. Afterwards, Shadi comments that they must not trust him or sympathise with him. He asks Fadwa to contact her friends in the square and ask them to return to their homes immediately. Shadi is convinced that the President will gather the greatest number of people possible together and will seize them in order to offer them as a sacrifice to the devil. There is, indeed, a large number of hostages with him now, and the people should all stay in their homes so that Shadi can find a means to save them. Fadwa, who notices her father surreptitiously wiping tears from his eyes, indulges him.

On the morning of the following day, Shadi has not slept, as is normal for him these days. He is crying hard and begs Fadwa not to leave the house. He kneels down to kiss her feet. Fadwa sits on a chair in the living room and tells him that she will not go out, in compliance with his wishes. She takes advantage of his going to the bathroom and leaves quickly and closes the door behind her.

After midday, The Battle of the Camels begin. Fadwa follows the events from her workplace and she receives calls and pleas for help from the square. She moves around, she comes and goes, and through all that, tears keep pouring down her face until, in time, she forgets that she is crying.

At sunset, she replies to her father who has called her on her mobile. She hears him start to cry, she takes a breath and says: "Have you seen, Dad, what the heathen sons of dogs have done?!... Never mind, Dad, the blood of those people will not be wasted." Her father's voice on the other end is breaking up. He tells her that he is crying for the sake of her brother, who ran away from him when he was trying to take him to the doctor in accordance with the plan that he had agreed with her. Her father tells her that her brother is now missing altogether, he does not have an ID card on him, nor a mobile – not even any small change in his pocket. Her father begs her for help, saying that he doesn't know what he should do. Fadwa takes her handbag and leaves the radio station in a hurry without even asking permission. She gets in her car and drives around the streets searching for Shadi. She calls her father – who is also out searching – from time to time.

She drives around the main roads and narrow side streets of Ayn Shams where Rim, his ex-girlfriend, lives. At three in the morning she is driving her car along Rameses Street when a friend of hers calls to tell her about a sniper and countless deaths and injuries. Fadwa gets out close to the Ghamra metro station and sits on the pavement. She slaps her face several times. Fadwa smacks herself and screams, her tears mingle with her snot in the pitch-dark of the completely empty street. Her mobile rings again. Her father asks her to come back home and tells her that Shadi is now with him and that they are on their way to the hospital.

Fadwa will learn from her father when he returns that the army contacted him to ask him if he knew anyone called Shadi and requested that he head for the airport immediately to take him back. When Shadi arrives, the father finds him barefoot. His clothes are ripped and he has multiple wounds. He will learn from the captain that he was beaten up by people in the Sheraton compound who thought that he was off his head, and the army only managed to rescue him from

their hands by the skin of their teeth, realising belatedly that he was not fully in his right mind, and were able by some miracle to find out his name and the mobile number that they called him on.

The father gets in the car after helping the exhausted Shadi to stretch out on the back seat. The captain, speaking only to him, says: "Take good care of him, Hajj, it would be a shame to let someone in that state out on his own in these troubled times." The father wipes away a tear that he can't fight back and takes Shadi to the hospital.

Neither the father nor Fadwa know that Shadi fled from his father in the morning in order to rescue Fadwa, who had been detained with the hostages when she went out that morning. The hostages were all together in the Al-Fateh mosque and the President's men kept smuggling them from mosque to mosque to prevent Shadi, their saviour, from arriving to rescue them. They finally came to a stop in a mosque in the Sheraton compound and Shadi managed to trick his way into it before it was evacuated at the time of evening prayer. The hostages were praying at the time, pleading with Allah to rescue them from the situation they were in. Shadi interrupted their prayers and freed them all. He punched some of them, but that didn't matter because it was all for their →

ABOVE: The Battle of the Camels, when supporters of the then President Hosni Mubarak attacked protestors on Tahrir Square with metal weapons, heavy rocks and Molotov cocktails, 1 February 2011

→ benefit at the end of the day. When Shadi was sure they had all left the mosque and were safe, he finally left the mosque himself and was met outside by the dogs of State Security wearing plain clothes. They showered blows down on him, then handed him over to the Republican Guard who, in their turn, gave him a good beating. When Rim learnt from her family what was happening to him, she asked the devil to call his soldiers off him and threatened that otherwise she would desert him. The devil acquiesced to her command, and requested that the President let Shadi go, so the

President immediately gave an order to the Republican Guard to phone his father so that he could come and take charge of him.

A week later, on the Thursday, Fadwa would receive leaked information, in the course of her work, of a report that the President had stepped down that night. She hurriedly finishes her work and decides to go home to listen to the speech with her father so that they can share in the joy together.

At twenty minutes to ten at night, she is downloading a set of the most famous patriotic songs onto her computer at home. She connects a speaker to the computer, and decides that the celebration will be loud and last until dawn.

After the speech, Fadwa was trying to stand up, but she just couldn't. She thought of calling out for her father, then gave up the idea, out of pity for his state of health. She told herself that that was the last thing he needed. She kept quiet, and after several minutes she tried again to stand up, but she still couldn't do it. She burst into silent tears, after which she fell asleep where she was, sitting on the chair. She felt her father waking her up and leading her to her bed. She wanted to know what the time was, but she could not see the clock, she was just focused on the fact that she was actually walking now with her father.

Her father tells her that her brother is now missing altogether, he does not have an ID card on him, nor a mobile

---

The following day she sees a brilliant video on the computer telling the story of the events of the revolution from the very beginning. She feels deeply moved and tears run down her face. She prays: "Oh, Lord, we did what we had to do, now you must play your part, oh Lord." Her father is sitting in the living room watching terrestrial TV, when she hears a collective roar from the street and the neighbours, like the one you hear when the national team scores a goal in an African Nations Cup match. She runs out to the living room and finds her father prostrate, crying, on the floor. She follows with unbelieving eyes the breaking news titles on the TV reporting the news of the resignation. She starts to jump up and down like a crazy woman. She is yelling, believing that she is trilling cries of joy, but she doesn't know how to do that so she just keeps on yelling. Her father watches her, sitting on the floor, and laughs amid his tears.

She prances back to the computer and starts playing the patriotic songs that she downloaded yesterday, at top volume. She dances, she jumps and carries on shouting, her father comes into her room, smiling at her, dancing with her, then hugs her and cries.

The following day, in the afternoon, when Fadwa has finished getting dressed, she goes out, accompanied by her father, to bring Shadi back from the hospital, where he has spent ten

$\rightarrow$

→ days receiving intensive treatment. Shadi is calm now. His face is bloated from so much sleep and he has almost zero ability to concentrate because of the high dosage of strong medication that he has been on.

Once home, Shadi sits in front of the TV. He watches for himself the resignation speech, which all the channels are broadcasting on continuous repeat. Fadwa sits at his side. He laughs and points at the man standing behind Omar Suleiman and says to Fadwa: "Why is that man there doing that?"

Fadwa notices for the first time the man with his scowling face and suspicious penetrating glances, and she laughs too.

Shadi asks her about dinner and she tells him that they will get a Kentucky Fried Chicken takeaway tonight. He asks her to order the 68-piece meal for him and she laughs and tells him that she's ordered the 116-piece one for him, then he laughs too.

After a few minutes they watch the speech, which is being shown again. Shadi looks contemplatively at Omar Suleiman then turns to Fadwa, saying: "Can you believe it? That Suleiman was using

---

Her father is sitting in the living room watching terrestrial TV, when she hears a collective roar from the street and the neighbours, like the one you hear when the national team scores a goal in an African Nations Cup match

---

black magic too?" Fadwa looks aghast and the delight drains from her face, indeed her right eye flickers in a nervous movement that she can't control. Shadi observes her reaction and bursts out laughing and says: "I'm kidding you, you idiot." She smiles slowly and cautiously, and his giggles grow louder and he repeats it to her, struggling to breathe from his laughter. "I swear to God, and even on the life of our father." She contemplates his non-stop laughter, then she laughs too, until tears fill her eyes, and the sound of their intermingled laughter fills the space of the living room.

....

This is an extract of Laugh and the World Laughs with Me. The full short story will appear on indexoncensorship.org in July

Translated by Sue Copeland

Eman Abdelrahim *is an Egyptian short-story writer best known for her collection Rooms and Other Stories. One of her stories appears in The Book of Cairo, published by Comma Press*

NEW ARABIC LITERATURE
FROM SAQI BOOKS

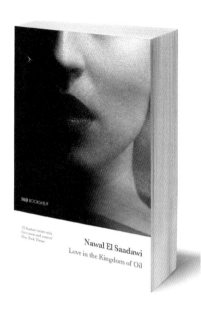

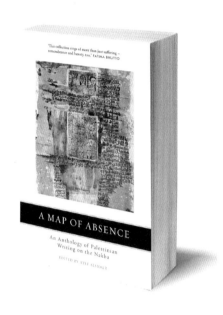

Love in the Kingdom of Oil
Nawal El Saadawi

'At a time when nobody
else was talking, [El
Saadawi] spoke the
unspeakable.'
Margaret Atwood

The Quarter
Naguib Mahfouz

'A master of both
detailed realism and
fabulous storytelling'
The Guardian

A Map of Absence:
An Anthology of
Palestinian Writing
on the Nakba
Atef Alshaer

'A crucial anthology'
Molly Crabapple

Now Available from all Good Bookshops

www.saqibooks.com

Speak out, shut out

Index staff have been out and about talking to people from all over the world about how they overcome obstacles to free expression. **Lewis Jennings** reports

48(02): 96/99 | DOI: 10.1177/0306422019857916

"**I**DENTITY IS IN some ways like a toothache," said Palestinian writer Iyad el-Baghdadi. "You are not normally aware of your teeth, but you become aware when your tooth aches. You are not normally aware of your identity until you are stripped of it."

He was speaking at the Ifex conference in Berlin, which was also attended by Index CEO Jodie Ginsberg, who asked: "What is the response of the international community when your own country rejects you? It's not something we think about."

El-Baghdadi is an activist who rose to prominence during the Arab Spring. He was forcibly exiled by the United Arab Emirates in 2014 for his online outspokenness against repression and leadership in the region – namely against the government of Egypt for playing a part in the ousting of former President Mohamed Morsi and the violent crackdowns that followed.

El-Baghdadi says that people in some Arab countries turn to social media because "if they want to go to protest they are shot before they do so".

In an ironic turn of events, el-Baghdadi was later not allowed to board a Ryanair flight from Berlin to Dublin. He was told this was because of his refugee status, despite the Irish government website stating that his entrance would be permitted. Not one to be silenced, he used Twitter to call out the airline and was eventually allowed on the flight. He received an apology from Ryanair.

Ginsberg found el-Baghdadi inspiring. She said he was particularly powerful when he talked about the responsibility of countries round the world to protect individuals who are rejected from their own country.

A recurring theme at the Ifex conference, which brought together human rights organisations and activists from around the world, was the challenge to free expression online.

Ginsberg said this was a particular issue in countries where governments used social media to engage in hate speech or to incite hate towards minority groups.

"We have to work out the balance between protecting freedom of expression online but

@IndexCensorship @Index_Magazine
Thanks to our hosts University of Essex and partners Essex Book Festival

CREDIT: Elina Kansikas (top right),Lewis Jennings (bottom right)

ensuring the government is not abusing its power to shut down the speech and rights of minority groups," she said. "If these people are bullied off social media, we have lost."

Also this quarter, Index magazine editor Rachael Jolley was at the International Journalism Festival in Perugia, Italy. Attended by some of the magazine's contributors from around the world, one of the discussions was about how online spaces could offer platforms for the

You are not normally aware of your identity until you are stripped of it

media when others were closed off.

"Wana Udobang talked about how it's hard to publish in the traditional media for Nigerian journalists who want to write stories that are sometimes controversial. They will find internet spaces that are less controlled," she said.

"Kaya Genç talked about how social media is one of the ways Turkish journalists get their stories out. It's important to have the opportunity to hear people's personal experiences first-hand and get up-to-date with some of the obstacles they are finding. When you go to a conference, it's quite often just people from one continent, so to get that kind of overlapping of what's going on in different parts of the world at the same time is unusual.

"You really hear from journalists operating from all over the world, and I think that's →

ABOVE: Zehra Doğan gives a heartfelt speech at the Freedom of Expression Awards 2019, alongside fellowship and advocacy officer Perla Hinojosa

LEFT: Editor Rachael Jolley chairs a discussion at Essex Book Festival alongside actors from the Globe to Globe tour Phoebe Fildes and Matthew Romain

CREDIT: Elina Kansikas (top left,bottom left) International Journalism Festival (opposite)

Some panellists had difficulty speaking because they were so moved by the terrible experiences that colleagues, and they themselves, have had

from personal experiences, which was very compelling. At one point, some panellists had difficulty speaking because they were so moved by the terrible experiences that colleagues, and they themselves, have had," said Hyvarinen. "It paints a scary picture for journalists. Generating good will and pressuring governments is key moving forward. There's a need for countries to clean up their own house and we have to act."

→ really rare. There were some incredibly brave people who are doing journalism in incredibly difficult circumstances." Head of advocacy Joy Hyvarinen took part in a conference entitled "Journalists Under Attack: a threat to media freedom", at the Organisation for Security and Co-operation in Europe in Vienna. Alessandro Azzoni, the Italian ambassador to the OSCE, joined prominent journalists and freedom of expression advocates on the panel, which was moderated by Hyvarinen.

They discussed the threats to journalists in the 57 OSCE countries, including those in the European Union. "Many journalists who were there spoke

ABOVE: Jodie Ginsberg introduces the Freedom of Expression Awards 2019

Perla Hinojosa, Index's fellowships and advocacy officer, has been highlighting the introduction of a new rule – Decree 349 – in Cuba that would mean all artists having their work pre-approved by the Ministry of Culture. She was part of a protest at London's Tate Modern against its introduction.

A previous fellow of Index's Freedom of Expression Awards, Luis Manuel Otero Alcántara, who runs Havana's Museum of Dissidence, has been part of the fight against Decree 349. As this magazine went to press, he had been arrested three times for taking part in protests.

Index made a statement, along with Pen International and Artists at Risk Connection, to voice support for Alcantara and other independent Cuban artists.

"It's important for cultural expression to survive because that's the heart of any country's identity," said Hinojosa.

She added that Cuba's constant attempts to censor artists whose opinions did not line up with those of the government were hindering such expression.

"Artists are being harassed, their families are being targeted, and so the consequences of Decree 349 are bad," she said. "In order to help, we need to bring light to the decree and how it hinders artistic free expression."

She also asked people to share the statement and to tweet about it using #NoAlDecreto349.

"It's important for Index to show solidarity because I think there's this romanticism of socialist governments, or Cuba in itself, and I think a lot of people don't actually know what goes on in these countries," she said. "These artists are seen as dissidents, but in reality they are just expressing their needs."

In March, Helen Galliano, head of strategic events and partnerships, attended the Essex Book Festival, where Index hosted Unspeakable, a series of debates and workshops.

One discussion, chaired by Index editor Rachael Jolley and featuring actors from the Globe Theatre, who completed a two-year world tour performing Shakespeare, shed light on theatre censorship.

"Theatre uses analogies and metaphors a lot, so you don't always have to be talking directly about the subject or the issue," Galliano said. "You can use it to find ways around potential censors or regimes.

"It's really exciting to hear the actors' stories, as quite often we don't have the opportunity to hear about the inner workings of a play and everything that goes with that." ⊗

Lewis Jennings is Index's editorial assistant and the 2018 Tim Hetherington fellow

ABOVE: Kaya Genç, Rachael Jolley, Caroline Muscat and Wana Udobang together on a panel during the International Journalism Festival in Perugia, Italy

LEFT: Mimi Mefo, a winner of the Freedom of Expression Awards 2019, chats to guests at the ceremony held in The May Fair Hotel, London

END NOTE

Hanging truth out to dry

The new trend in film propaganda is all about undermining the public's belief in the truth. **Sally Gimson** talks to film-maker **Maxim Pozdorovkin**

48(02): 100/104 | DOI: 10.1177/0306422019857917

WE ARE BEING carpet-bombed by false information so we do not know what is true and what is not. It's deliberate, and that is what propaganda looks like today.

This is the view of award-winning documentary maker Maxim Pozdorovkin, whose film Our New President followed the disinformation campaign in Russia during the 2016 US presidential election. It was shown this spring at the British Film Institute in London as part of a series marking 30 years of the internet called Born Digital: Raised by the Internet.

He told Index: "The tactic of modern-day propaganda… it's disorientation… creating inconsistency is the point. It is creating the sort of situation where there is a sense of erosion in the ability even to figure out what is true."

Pozdorovkin is of Russian-Armenian heritage. He was brought up in the Soviet Union in the 1980s and moved to the USA when he was 10 years old. He made his reputation with a documentary, Pussy Riot, A Punk Prayer, which followed the imprisonment and trial of the Russian punk band Pussy Riot.

"The way that Russia has won [the information war] is by undermining the institutional trust, which is a fundamentally different thing from making people believe that communism was better or that [President Vladimir] Putin is a great bringer of peace, or whatever it is," he said.

He argues that, historically, propaganda has often focused on governments putting out strategic disinformation while pretending to be truthful, particularly during wartime: a government making a film about a battle advance or victory it has won.

Pozdorovkin describes how Nazi propagandist Joseph Goebbels spent a lot of money on making newsreels of real events. According to the US newsreel expert Raymond Fielding,

WORLD LEADERS ON TWITTER

World leaders with the most Twitter followers as of May 2018

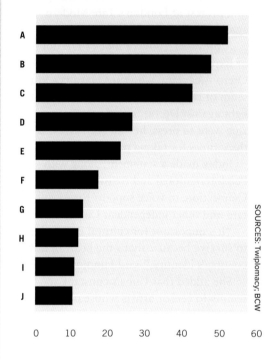

SOURCES: Twiplomacy; BCW

KEY

A Donald Trump, US @RealDonaldTrump *
B Pope Francis, Vatican @Pontifex
C Narendra Modi, India @NarendraModi *
D Narendra Modi, India @PMOIndia **
E President, US @POTUS **
F The White House, US @WhiteHouse
G Recep Tayip Erdoğan, Turkey @RT_Erdogan
H Sushma Swaraj, India @SushmaSwaraj
I Queen Rania, Jordan @QueenRania
J Joko Widodo, Indonesia @Jokowi

* Personal account. ** Institutional account.

CREDIT: Third Party Films

for instance, Goebbels sent 300 cameramen to film the German invasion of Norway in 1939, while the British sent just one. The German newsreels, made in the style of the famous British Pathé News, were then manipulated with music and a voiceover to put out pro-Nazi messages.

Now, he argues, the objective of a government such as Russia's is to provide and encourage so much information that it is increasingly impossible for the public to disentangle what is real from what is not.

"It's more about turning the media or the internet space into a garbage dump. It's little bit like carpet-bombing," said Pozdorovkin.

Pozdorovkin's film won the World Cinema Documentary Special Jury Award for Editing at the Sundance Festival last year. The documentary uses clips from the internet to make the hour-and-a-quarter-long documentary about the US presidential campaign. The boast of the film is that nothing in it is true.

His objective was to make a film "about Kremlin news about what we call the federal channels".

He wanted the audience to experience propaganda and "fake news" rather than have it explained. The election itself was simply a backdrop which provided a story that everyone knew.

"Not a single one of those people had come from America. The only thing they knew about America was from television – you can make it this hermetically-sealed chamber of disinformation," said Pozdorovkin.

The documentary is a collage of video footage. Some of it was taken from Russian television, especially Russia 1, Russia Today and NTV, and it features the Russian TV host and propagandist Dmitry Kiselev. Other footage is

from YouTube videos which ordinary people have made – and include clips of people wearing masks of silver foil and someone sticking pins into a homemade doll of Hillary Clinton.

The film's name comes from the amateur video of a little boy who watches Donald Trump being elected on television and believes that Trump is somehow Russia's new president.

While this may seem daft, Robert Mueller, special counsel at the US Department of Justice, has spent millions of dollars →

ABOVE: Poster for the documentary Our New President

→ investigating allegations that there was co-ordination between Trump's presidential campaign and the Russian government.

And that, said Pozdorovkin, is what should make us suspicious – that, ultimately, liberals in America are promoting and hoping for the same narrative as the Kremlin, that Trump is working with the Russians.

It is, he says, important to emphasise the media hyperbole at work and he wanted to show with the video clips in his film what he calls the "role and logic" of spectacle and the corruption of the media. "That is the disease which has spread from Russia," he said.

In a time when the debate is about what Facebook and other social media platforms should do about "fake news", this insight shows that dealing with it is a lot more complicated than legislators would like us to believe.

In the UK, for instance, the government's Online Harms White Paper seeks to tackle disinformation whether intentionally harmful or not.

What Pozdorovkin is suggesting is that the problem is the slew of information generated. There are a lot of ordinary people, including children, using a theatrical medium such as YouTube to disseminate information, and it is

It is creating the sort of situation where there is a sense of erosion in the ability even to figure out what is true

unclear whether even they believe what they are saying.

The other insight Pozdorovkin offers is that pieces of information multiply themselves because of the algorithms on sites such as Google and Facebook.

He says that if you create a piece of content, for a few seconds it is competitive with entrenched sites such as The New York Times. If you create that content often enough, some of it will get through. It is the theory of troll factories, and he says "all internet revenue streams are based on that".

Meanwhile, propaganda footage from RT is free to use on YouTube, unlike US and British broadcast material from CNN or the BBC, which is protected for commercial reasons and difficult to rip off. This means anyone can use RT clips to create cheap blogs and memes using footage which appears to be reliable because of the high production values applied.

And add to all this the fact that the metric now used with news is whether something is liked or disliked or whether it gets a thumbs-up or a thumbs-down on social media. That means, says Pozdorovkin, that someone such as Trump becomes "the most popular leader in history by a landslide" because likes and follows is how success is judged in the world of information. Indeed, research carried out in May 2018 showed Trump's personal account had 52 million Twitter followers – more than any other leader in the world. He has 60 million today compared to the Indian Prime Minister Narendra Modi's 47 million.

Pozdorovkin is fascinated by this use of media. For his PhD, he studied early newsreels made by the famous Russian →

BELOW: YouTube clip used in the documentary Our New President showing a Russian boy celebrating the election of Donald Trump

CREDIT: Third Party Films

A new spellbinding story of modern China by the bestselling author of *The Good Women of China*

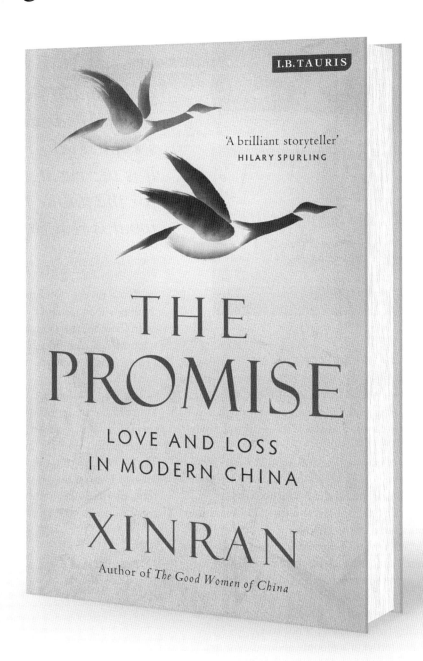

At the start of the 20th century in China, the Hans were married in an elaborate ceremony before they were even born. They went on to have nine children, though fate, and the sweep of 20th-century history, would later divide them.

Describing the lives and loves of this extraordinary family over four generations, this moving story paints a crucial and intimate portrait of modern China's extraordinary century.

288 pages • 216 x 138mm • HARDBACK • £17.99 • 9781788313629

I.B. TAURIS   Bloomsbury.com

ABOVE: Documentary director Maxim Pozdorovkin

The objective of a government such as Russia's is to provide and encourage so much information that it is increasingly impossible for the public to disentangle what is real from what is not

→ documentary maker Dziga Vertov after the October 1917 Russian revolution. Vertov later went on to make the classic silent documentary Man with a Movie Camera about Soviet urban life.

It's perhaps not surprising that he believes film is a more powerful propaganda weapon than the printed page. And Russians, he maintains, are still more sceptical of what they read than of what they see.

"What I find is that while Russians are more sceptical of print-based media, at the visual level they are much more gullible," he said, citing the footage in his documentary which appears to show an assassination attempt on Trump (which, again, is not true).

Pozdorovkin is gloomy about the future. The objective of those who coordinate this propaganda, he says, is to undermine the hegemony of the West. People such as Kiselev believe that anything that upsets the balance is a "net good".

He thinks that the only way to combat this new form of propaganda is to make people more media-literate.

But he is worried about the social conclusions which young people draw from what they see, and, for him, a distressing element of the Hillary Clinton/Trump election story was the conclusion of the video of the boy

he found on the YouTube who thinks Donald Trump is Donald Duck.

In the film, the Donald Duck boy says that what he has seen on television about Clinton proves that a woman can never be president of the USA.

Pozdorovkin said: "What this kid thinks about Hillary Clinton doesn't matter. What this kid thinks about women will have direct consequences on the women around him. That's the core of it all. He takes this thing he sees on TV, randomly, with some authority and then internalises it and broadens it out into this pseudo-intellectual position." ⊗

Sally Gimson is the deputy editor of Index on Censorship

CREDIT: Ksenia Poulber

CORStIONS

CORRECTIONS

||||||||||||||||||||||||||||||||||||||||||||||||||||

Issue 48.01, Is this all the local news?

News loses, page 20

In this article we quoted The New York Times political reporter Kate Zernicki. The reporter we were referring to is Kate Zernike and an editing error later referred to her as "he". We apologise for any confusion.